THE UNRELENTING LEADER

Practical Leadership Lessons Through Challenging Times

All rights reserved. No part book may not be reproduced, duplicated, or transmitted without direct written permission from the author or the publisher. This book is copyright protected and for personal use only. You cannot edit, distribute, sell, use, quote, or paraphrase any part of this book without the author or publisher's consent.

© Copyright 2021

TABLE OF CONTENTS

ACKNOWLEDGMENTS

To all the everyday leaders out there, you are the unsung heroes of leadership, mentorship, and true change in the world. Keep doing what you can to grow and develop not only yourselves but also your teams.

To all of my supervisors and bosses, thank you. You've taught me what it means to be an effective leader.

And finally to Alisha. Your strength of character, beautiful soul, and dedication to push me to be better have been a guiding light through all my troubles.

INTRODUCTION

A PERSONAL EXPERIENCE WITH POST-TRAUMATIC STRESS DISORDER

My personal experience with post-traumatic stress disorder started on January 28th, 2008, while I was deployed to northern Iraq in a town called Mosul. I was part of a United States Air Force unit. Their individual members were divided into Weapons Intelligence Teams and attached to the Army as part of a troop augmentation program. We usually responded to areas where Improvised Explosive Devices (IEDs) detonated to conduct post-blast analysis, determine all the different components used in the bomb's creation, and figure out the enemy's next move. You can think of it as a type of forensic investigator in combat zones.

On this particular day, we rolled out to a scene where there was an underbelly blast. Good soldiers were lost instantly to the blast (I know three of them personally). When the bomb detonated (about three hundred pounds of explosive weight), it cut through the cab. We were carrying out a post-blast analysis of the area and walking through the scene, picking up pieces of body parts, body armor, and helmets of these gentlemen who would never go back to see their families again.

The devastation was shocking; the blast was so powerful that it threw the engine compartment and part of the cab of the up-armored vehicle over a kilometer away. I discovered later that the Intel provided to the team who was stuck was lacking in accuracy about the number and type of IEDs on that route. Someone who briefed them didn't do their job appropriately, and others paid the ultimate price. My issues with post-traumatic stress disorder started there and then. But I wouldn't really experience it until I came back from Iraq.

The analysts didn't take care of the guys outside of the wire, and that was what really got me into focusing a lot on what it means to be a leader; taking care of people, making sure they have what they need in order to carry out missions and execute tasks. I believe we are here for more than ourselves. We are here for each other. It's not about me; it's about "we."

To date, I still wake up with nightmares and cold sweats. But I believe that part of the lessons I learned through this post-traumatic stress disorder is the best way I can cope as a leader is to take the best team care I can of my team; people underneath me and above me, and around me. They'd do the same for me. The reason I do what I do is because I love the people I work with; I love the men and women and the team that I'm around.

I had a lot of trouble going to open areas where there are a lot of crowds, and I have to sit constantly facing the door and make sure that nobody can sneak up on it. In a high-stress situation, my heart starts pounding really hard, and I had to learn how to calm myself down a little and tell myself that it's okay and everything's going to be alright.

Leading through these stressful times as a leader, especially at a higher level in an organization, I've realized that stress is constant, and the pressure we put on ourselves is much. However, I think we could mitigate better and help others not make the same mistake I made, putting stress where it doesn't need to be.

The Concept Of Leadership From A Personal Perspective

The topic and concept of leadership are among the most discussed topics in the corporate world today, and rightly so. As a result of this, many opinions, concepts, and strategies have been generated about the subject, which sometimes makes it hard for people who want to practice active Leadership to learn and thrive. Many have argued that leaders are born and not made; others are of the opinion that some people are born leaders, while others believe that some leaders have leadership thrust upon them as a result of circumstances.

Often, Leadership has been idealized, discussed, and described as a tricky thing, making it seemingly unattainable for anyone who wants to become a great leader. Regardless of the category or opinions generated about Leadership, it is certain that all leaders share a certain attribute that makes them leaders worthy of being followed. In fact, you will find that most people already possess these attributes and are likely to develop them and teach others till you become a complete leader. This book, therefore, seeks to help leaders who intend to improve in terms of these attributes to scale and advance their careers and lives.

Have you ever felt the urge to be better, improve and advance in life and your career, especially as a leader? Well, you are not alone, as even the greatest of leaders have always felt this way. In fact, I can boldly say that you started reading this book with the intention of improving and getting better, to begin with. This desire or urge is usually what precedes change and improvement, which is necessary for cultivating the necessary skills needed to advance in your life and career. Most times, leaders are overwhelmed by the challenges they are faced with and often question their capabilities. This has led to leaders having to cope with the demands of their role and navigating through the doubts or desires, which has spurred them to seek advancement and development in Leadership in the first place.

This book focuses on helping people see the value in themselves and others so that they are empowered and excited to bring their best to life every day.

PART ONE

LEADERSHIP AS A TEAM ENDEAVOR

CHAPTER ONE

OVERVIEW OF LEADERSHIP

The greatest impact on humanity is leadership. It is the key to our advancement and the peak of what one can accomplish. We've achieved all that we've achieved due to the leadership of individuals who saw a need or problem, fought for an answer or solution, and inspired others to do the same. Leadership is what keeps us moving forward. To make the world move in the right direction, all we need to do is lead.

Definition Of Leadership

Defining leadership can be difficult, and defining yourself as a leader is as well. I want to inspire and motivate those around me, whether they are colleagues, friends, or peers, to challenge past long-held beliefs that could hold them back from realizing their potential.

Leadership can be a confounding term and defined subjectively. If you ask ten people what leadership means, you'll most likely get ten different answers.

Simply put, leadership can be defined as doing the right thing to motivate and inspire others towards achieving a certain goal. The right thing guides leaders to make the choices they make. Most leaders do what's right by bringing in the right people to help them.

In a more comprehensive term, leadership is instilling a cause in others. Let's break that down below:

First, leaders instill a desire to focus efforts toward a common goal. This is often a result of leaders creating a shared vision or concept for all to fundamentally believe and support. While some may have to be convinced about the vision, they must never be coerced. Leadership isn't an automatic authority. This suggests that executives, managers, commanders, and the likes aren't leaders by default. You can make someone smile, but you cannot tell them to feel happy. Similarly, if you tell someone to do something, but if that person doesn't believe the cause, their efforts toward what you've told them to do would eventually come to nothing. They have to *want* to do it, to be intrinsically motivated to do so.

The next is "cause." This is usually a vision or concept that results in some result or change. People follow this cause because they believe in an underlying concept it promotes. We battle dirt not because we, as humans, are designed to bath but due to its negative impacts on our lives. If no real result or changes occur from the cause, then people will be hesitant to follow it or not follow it at all.

The last is "others." Leaders need followers to be leaders. This probably seems obvious, but it's not uncommon for somebody to carry a cause upon their shoulders. If they never share that cause, it will eventually die with them. Leadership isn't a solo endeavor; it is a team sport-no one can lead on his or her own. Regardless of how impactful an accomplishment could be, all of it will be for nothing without others to hold on to the cause.

When we integrate all of these elements into a single definition, we will get something like: Leadership is instilling a cause in others." This might sound simple, but it is powerful. It illustrates that our strength is in one another. People can carry a cause on their own as far as others support them. When we have the support of others, our efforts can have a lasting impact. Science, business, religion, and politics-we follow and sustain the causes of leaders in all aspects of life when their visions are instilled in us.

The Truth About Leadership

One of the difficult truths of leadership is that it's a moving target. It is an endless and dynamic learning process/experience that spans your entire life. Many valuable insights and perspectives are shared to help us master a number of things to become leaders.

These include passion, purpose, empathy, communication, or any other thing considered a leader's positive traits. I have found great joy and knowledge in these things but have also come to understand they are all parts of the general picture that leadership entails. To fulfill the leadership insights and perspectives, one must know the whole picture. This is the truth about leadership.

BECOMING A LEADER

Anyone can become a leader, but not anyone can become a leader at any time. The aspects of our lives could different turns and need different priorities. When one aspect needs more attention, it gets that attention at the expense of other aspects, putting us in a precarious position. To become a leader, we must first understand the hierarchy of leadership.

The Leadership Hierarchy

After a keen scrutinizing of what makes a leader, it is clear that no aspect of leadership can stand alone. Believing that it could stand alone would be to ignore one's humanity and how our experiences are shaped and efforts are impacted. The challenge is determining what is needed to support our leadership life. The concept of building upon needs isn't new, and it is the groundwork that sets the tone for leadership hierarchy.

Maslow's Hierarchy of Needs

Abraham Maslow's Hierarchy of Needs has been a great theory in assessing human behavior for many years. For people who don't know what the theory entails, it focuses on the thought of motivational growth and the need to satisfy that growth repose on one another. If one need suffers, it impacts all of the needs above it.

Much has been said and debated about Maslow's Hierarchy. I won't re-evaluate most of that here. I would say that Maslow's Hierarchy isn't completely cut-and-dry prescriptive, as you would expect anything that broadly summarizes human behavior. Its simplicity (including the pyramid form that it took overtime) is a way to help others know It as an equivalent of the true leadership hierarchy.

The Leadership Path

Maslow's hierarchy focuses on the need of the individual and acts as a foundation for one's motivation and growth. But not all people become leaders. There is something beyond the individual which spurs that next step. That thing is the leadership Path.'

The Leadership Path is a hierarchy of its own, made from three layers that depend on one another. It is no coincidence that the Leadership Path is a reflection of the form of Maslow's Hierarchy. While Maslow's Hierarchy is a representation of the individual culminating in self-realization, the Leadership Path is a representation of that individual's focus expanding into society. Our nature is to socialize and work as a team. The Leadership Path believes that change is the only key to the ever-expanding impact of a single person on society. The structural layers of the leadership path are Engagement, Influence, and Leadership.

Let's take a look at each of them below:

Engagement: The first layer of the Leadership Path, engagement, occurs when a cause has been instilled in an individual—this alignment results in commitment and accountability to this cause. Individuals begin performing well in support of the cause and continuously grow to believe and serve it.

Engagement is a popular topic in leadership. It has been established that engaged employees perform better, leading a business to outperform their competitors, achieve higher earnings, innovate more, improve turnover, and so on. This outcome is true for engagement with any cause, whether it is in the business environment or not. Engaged individuals work harder and perform better because they really care.

Influence: As illustrated earlier, one isn't really a leader when they do things alone. For an individual's efforts to expand and persist, people must be brought into the fold. This is often done naturally and effectively through influence.

Becoming an influencer means establishing trust with people that would support the cause. This is usually done through transparency and collaboration, which let others know they are important for achieving success. Influencers also inspire through a mix of humility and confidence. They look for ideas to the best course of action and make the choices toward those actions, even when the ideas came from somebody else. While they use humility and confidence to make decisions, they use self-compassion to balance their ego, be comfortable and forgiving of themselves for making mistakes, and to further inspire others to do the same.

This layer is where numerous would-be usually leaders fail. Often, power is established before a person has had the opportunity to put any of the traits into practice. This results in an authority that's seemingly easier to wield, but that doesn't result in long-term success. When authority takes over, it becomes the main target over the cause itself.

Leadership: This is the final layer in leading others by instilling the cause in them and teaching them the way to follow the same path to leadership. By aligning others to the cause, it's furthered beyond what the individual could accomplish. The leader must empower and encourage others through the engagement and influence layers, bringing them to the leadership layer, perpetuating the cycle, and multiplying efforts for the cause. This also means the individual is no longer alone in being responsible for supporting the cause. The multiplication of leaders through the Leadership Path takes the cause from being an individual effort to having a life of its own.

The Cause Inflection Point

Using the Leadership Path, anyone can become a leader in any area, but that doesn't mean that following the trail will make one a leader in everything. Leadership happens in the willful pursuit of a cause. That time at which an individual connects with a cause-at which the individual of Maslow's Hierarchy connects with the Leadership Path-is referred to as'The Cause Inflection Point.'Whether that time is reached through self-discovery, outside motivators, or a leader instilling their own cause, the inflection point is the difference between undertaking a journey.

The Leader Hierarchy captures what it takes to become a true leader, whose causes are going to be adopted and carried on by others. However, perfection in executing each level of the hierarchy isn't necessary to motivate others. Indeed, such perfection isn't even possible. Leadership is a path, a continuous journey, not a destination, and the Leader Hierarchy is your compass to guide you on that path.

The True Leader

By nature, leaders need others to do as they do. Leaders have followers, or in other words, leaders have people around them who they are working with to instill leadership skills in them. Simply put, leaders are surrounded by other leaders.

I find it perplexing when so-called leaders try to compete with others around them or do everything on their own. Leaders who attempt to do all it all or be all on their own inadvertently set themselves up to fail.

A characteristic of true leadership is humility. Humility is a quality that allows a person to admit that not have all the answers. An individual with humility welcomes, appreciates and learns from what others can contribute.

There are several gifted people who could be incredible leaders. However, what holds them back is their desire to do it all on their own so that they can take all credit for their achievements.

This is unfortunate because nobody has the individual capacity that exceeds the capacity of the many people or a team. So why attempt to do the work of a team? Aside from the limited capacity, nobody has all the right ideas, either. Nobody has diverse enough skill sets to achieve a collective goal on their own. The standard required to even try to do everything or control everything by yourself is so high and almost impossible to meet.

This unfortunate attempt is usually seen when an individual feels the necessity to prove himself or herself. Below are some facts about leadership I've learned over the years that seemed counterintuitive to me at first:

Leadership Is Not Management: In the world today, people usually equate "leadership" and "management." We tend to acknowledge upper management because they are the leaders of our organization. But the very fact of the matter is that the two concepts have almost nothing in common. Good managers are often terrible leaders, and not every leader possesses the sensible skills to make a solid manager.

Leadership is often present at any level of any entity. That's one of the most important aspects of leadership: it is hospitable to everyone. All it takes is a willingness to listen to, genuinely care about, and deeply connect with our teams. This will go a long to boosting their morale and the capability to inspire others to maximize their potential.

The very notion of a leader places the responsibility on someone to lead the pack, motivate and guide the members of their team. But as mentioned earlier in this chapter, leadership isn't a solo endeavor. The purpose of leadership is acting through others. It can't be done or achieved all alone.

To effectively succeed as a leader, you need the capacity to empathize and identify with those around you. You need to look for and interact with unique individuals in unique ways to attach and collaborate with them effectively.

Leaders Should Be Learners: I mentioned this earlier, but it is worth repeating: leaders can never stop learning. There's no magical level of leadership goals you can attain that allows you to stop learning. Life is becoming more dynamic than ever; changing mindsets and innovative technologies, and new trends create an ever-evolving world for everyone. Leaders who don't plan to evolve along with the tide will be left stagnated.

Making a commitment to making yourself a leader is additionally a commitment to bettering those around you. If you are determined to become an efficient leader, don't ever let yourself become complacent.

Leadership Is Not All About The Leader: Leadership isn't about the leader alone, but it's only too easy to make it about them. Seeing leadership as being all about you will make you quickly lose track of its true meaning.

Below are some signs that can help you see if you're making leadership all about you.

1. **People rarely see or understand what people experience**: To resolve this, you have to be interested in what people are feeling, doing and thinking. This is part of being culturally and emotionally aware in your organization.

2. **You don't ask very many questions:** If you don't feel the impulse to ask people questions, it's a good indication that you only think about yourself. These aren't questions meant to stump someone so that you feel superior. Nor are these questions which are meant to glean one-word answers. The questions you should be asking are meant to deepen your understanding of the individuals on your teams, the culture, and how they all interact to keep the organization on track.

3. **You keep a list of your imperfections, weaknesses, and limitations:** This insecurity results in being overly critical of yourself, can only diminish your influence, weakens your relationships, and lowers your self-esteem. Knowing areas in which you're not the strongest or smartest is crucial to building healthy teams as it allows leaders to develop others and themselves by balancing strengths. However, hyper-focusing on the negative aspects can cause leaders and their teams to spiral to the point of inefficacy.

4. **Other people's abilities unsettle you:** If helping other people realize their potential is your goal, their strengths are your assets and the answer to your challenges. You don't have to be unsettled by their abilities or see them as competition. In fact, celebrate them! Thank them when they correct you because you just learned something new!

5. **You are in a constant crisis:** If this is your story, you need to go back and see the bigger picture and start leading and empowering others. Look, as humans, we tend to have "woe is me" moments from time to time, and that's okay for a bit. But if you're constantly in crisis mode, your focus is on you - not your teams or organization. Stepping back to see if the crisis you're in is truly a crisis may reveal it's simply a hiccup on the road to success. Reframe your thinking and turn this crisis point into a learning opportunity for yourself and share it with your teams.

6. **You are pessimistic about the future:** Leadership is about leading alone. It's about leading to a far better place. If you are pessimistic about the future, it would be difficult for you to

lead effectively.

7. **Reality is tedious for you**: If you can't see any opportunities, you've lost sight of the mission and purpose. You need to return to the drawing board and ask yourself why you want to lead. Create opportunities! You can't make an omelet without breaking some eggs, but find a hen if you don't have eggs.

CHAPTER TWO

TAKING RISKS

The fact that some leaders are more effective than others should not be a surprise to most. The formula for effectiveness is one that not very many have uncovered. However, being effective has so much to do with being a calculated risk-taker rather than someone who shies away from them. Taking a look at the most effective people in various sectors of the economy, we would realize a similar pattern between them. The pattern they all have in common is they are all risk-takers.

It is safe to say that the most effective leaders in the world are the ones who have a penchant for evaluating risky situations and combine it with their gut feeling (past experiences). Throughout history, there have been a lot of people that have risked it all. People like Bill Gates, Steve Jobs, Elon Musk, and Mark Zuckerberg all took risks to reach the heights they are today.

Unarguably, one of the best examples of effective risk-takers is Elon Musk, who risked it all on both Tesla and SpaceX. At one point, it appeared as if the risk he took would be the end of his entrepreneurial success story. Fortunately, it turned out well in the end, and today we see him as a prime example of an effective person.

Another of the world's most effective risk-taker, Mark Zuckerberg, founder of Facebook, once said that "the only strategy will certainly fail is not taking risks." This means that If you do not take any risks in your life, it means you are passing up all opportunities in front of you in favor of what you think is a stable future. That stability could be comforting, but it won't provide you with growth or advancement in any dimension, and ultimately, it will lead to failure.

In our quest to become leaders, we would definitely need to take risks. Leaders are risk-takers, but taking risks is not as easy or simple as it sounds. If you consistently risk, you are likely to fail at some point. This is something that will certainly happen. However, the question is not whether you will fail or not, but if you are smart enough to see why risking it all will help you become effective rather than playing it safe.

It is important to note that risk-takers do not succeed 100% of the time they take risks; however, their intuition usually pays off in the end. This is a balancing act that few master;

however if you are able to master this act, there is no telling how effective you can become.

You might be right if you think you have the same guts as the effective leaders we have mentioned above; however, you must recognize that risk-taking is a habit, not a talent or process, job or department. And also, remember that taking risks is all about having adequate knowledge of all the factors and putting them together into a calculated game plan. This shouldn't be done in a vacuum, though. Bring aboard individuals with experience in the applicable fields as needed.

Habits of leaders such as risk-taking can be developed, regardless of it being most deeply ingrained. As a result, it will take a lot of serious dedication and practice. Becoming an effective risk-taker is not for the faint-hearted. It requires a culture of willingness to fall forward and, many times, fail....sometimes on several attempts. The key to risk-taking for leaders is to encourage and to learn mindset from failure. We often don't try something new because of the fear of failure, but when leaders flip the script and help their teams view failure as a positive data point for learning, the whole organization grows.

Risks involve uncertainty and change; it is not just about taking blind gambles. Risks need to be calculated and involve challenging uncertainty and instituting change. If you have a desire to become a leader, it means you are at least a little unsatisfied with your present situation. Changing that situation entirely makes you more likely to escape it.

Unfortunately, a mere understanding of the benefits of risk-taking isn't enough. Most of us are naturally risk-averse; when we face a risk or a bad situation, the human brain is naturally built to imagine worst-case scenarios, which unfortunately stifles our productivity and makes us feel anxious and stressed, thereby discouraging us from taking risks.

What Are The Things That Make An Effective Risk-Taker?

Leaders, or to an extent, risk-takers, tend to demonstrate the following recognizable characteristics:

Goal-driven: Risks takers are goal-driven leaders. The sheer size of their goals motivates them to take calculated risks that will propel them to achieve said goals. They align their goals with their values and see the benefits of the journey.

Calculated seers: Risks takers know that it is not just about the immediate picture. They understand the bigger picture and do not make decisions in isolation or take things literally as they appear.

Conceptual thinking: Risk takers are able to apply experience and recognize patterns. They don't need all the information but aren't taking random guesses either. Instead, they merge the information they have at their disposal and merge it with their gut feelings to arrive at a decision.

Accountability: This is another characteristic of a risk-taker. They take full accountability for their actions and their outcomes as well as those of their teams. They do not play blame games when they fail to achieve their desired results.

Furthermore, here are some things you need to know about risks if you intend to become a leader:

Failure is an almost certainty when you take risks: Someone might ask, why do I have to take the risk when there is a probability of failure? The difference between taking risks and not taking risks is that while taking risks has a probability of failure, not taking risks is a certainty for failure. It's a part of life. Everything we engage has an element of failure attached to it. All successful leaders have different stories of failure linked to them. Thinking that your risk is will be pain-free and without stress is a pipedream; risk-taking comes with nightmares and pains.

There will be sleepless nights with insane nightmares of insecurity that leave you completely unnerved. This will certainly happen, no matter how positive you are about the risk you are about to take. The difference between good leaders and great leaders at this point is how they bounce back.

You have to stay true to yourself: Do not forget to stay true to yourself when taking risks. You cannot afford to take a risk and then turn into something you are not. This means you're not living by your values. It doesn't matter if you are risking a new relationship or new job opportunity; you must be yourself throughout the entire process. Don't pretend to be Elon Musk or Bill Gates, and you have no idea the nightmares they went through.

Risks are best taken with a clear head: You will live to regret your decision if you decide to take a risk when you are under duress, pressure, or any kind of external influence. Making decisions such as taking risks without a clear head will most likely result in failure. Hence when you have something important to decide, don't let your emotions take over your brain or cloud your sense of judgment.

You must fully understand what you are risking: Be certain that you have sufficient knowledge of the risk you are taking. Remember, risks should be calculated. Do not take a risk just because others are taking it, and it's working for them. If you believe the risk you want to take will be worth it or you have the necessary support you need from your friends or family, then go ahead and make the leap. If otherwise, seek more time and information and be certain before you take the risk.

You can fake a risk to take a risk: You can shape the way you think just by pretending that you are thinking in another way. A study conducted in 2016 found that people solved problems more creatively when they have the support of a risk-taking leader(ship). In other words, by thinking like a risk-taker and behaving like one, you can inevitably make you more comfortable with taking risks. Hence, you can be more comfortable taking risks simply by taking more risks (no matter how small) in your daily life.

PART TWO

LEADING TEAMS

CHAPTER THREE

CREATING A SAFE ENVIRONMENT TO FOSTER TRUST

Overview Of A Safe Environment

The necessity for people to feel safe and be themselves and take risks to achieve success is a clear requirement in today's world, but nurturing an individual's sense of safety is hard. A commitment to understanding this dynamic term means a leader must be able to create a safe environment for others to thrive.

Building an environment of genuine safety involves taking time to relate with followers on a personal level. But understanding the tricky dynamics of an individual's capacity for transformation might not be inherent or maybe seem realistic to all or any leaders. The first step to building a safe space for others is stepping away from productivity goals and connecting with the unique needs of people.

When leaders connect with subordinates, they will better engage in mutual affection and be more equipped to achieve trust. The responsibility is on the leader to earn the trust of their followers, and this is often nearly impossible if followers don't feel comfortable being themselves in their respective positions.

For example, let's assume Sammy is a member of an executive sales team is facing his first major hurdle at work. His sales input is the lowest he had overseen in more than a year. He approaches his boss, named Xavier, to ask for feedback regarding his performance with the sales update. He informs him that he has been unable to reach his sales target. Xavier, his boss, replies: "You need to meet your targets if you intend to keep your job with us."

Does this count as motivation? Not in any way. This is disparagement laced with the threat of the sack. Though such responses sometimes help to achieve short-term results, they'll eventually dissuade Sammy from long-term sustainable success because the threat of sack will constantly ring in his head.

Let us look at another scenario where Sammy is excelling and hitting all the organization's sales goals. When he turns in his sales update, Xavier tells his team, "Well, folks, this is usually what I like to see! Sammy can hit his targets, so why can't the rest of you do the same? Keep this performance up, Sammy!" after his statement, the team hesitantly applauses.

Does this sound better? The answer is no. In this instance, Xavier is just offering disparagement laced with a threat of sack to a team instead of recognizing their individual contributions. Not only do such tactics keep everyone jittery, even those that are top performers will feel less safe, and this means that they are less likely to trust intuition and take risks in their roles. In this second scenario, even Sammy may feel some extent of contention with his team because he is being defined by his comparison to them. This lowers the stakes for him and everybody else involved.

Leading with intimidation, using bullying tactics, or holding one's successes to castigate other team members will only end in disloyal employees who don't feel comfortable enough around their leader to efficiently problem-solve. Not only that, it means the leader is passing up a chance for sustainable growth.

It is possible that Sammy's challenges could get to her, but he could learn from his challenges and find himself as one of the most prolific salespeople on the team. Mistakes and challenges are, after all, the keys to building success. In the same view, when a team is asked to compete and compare, workers are often left feeling disenfranchised and lonely, and they may lose sight of common goals.

The Concept OfPsychological Safety

The concept of psychological safety can be found in almost all sectors. Psychological safety is about inclusivity and support. It doesn't mean forgiving poor performance or bad attitudes, but understanding that people are complex and psychologically nuanced. Each person has a unique attribute to contribute to his or her role, but nobody, especially not those in the workforce, will excel without trust, support, and confidence from those that lead.

Trust and respect are gained from sharing goals with mutual accountability, which enables employees or others to have a feeling about being part of a project, not merely an expendable resource. Accordingly, the continued challenge for leaders is finding the balance between recognizing individuals' unique strengths and acknowledging successes in a healthy, team-focused manner.

Trust As A Key To Building Safety

Trust transcends practical considerations. It involves feelings for employers, such as knowing that leaders are on "their side," and they will be treated fairly and with respect. In addition, setbacks will be viewed favorably or at least not viewed as outright negative.

Both sides of the trust coin impact a leader's ability to inspire and motivate employees. When people trust you, they need confidence in your decisions. Even in uncertainty, they need to be influenced by your leadership skills. That is because they believe you'll do what you say you will do.

Matching your words to your actions is a key component for building trust in the workplace and, ultimately, an organization's success. There are employees who believe that what leaders say and do has the biggest impact on their perception. When there's a disconnect between a leader's words and actions, employees are less likely to be committed and engaged to the organization.

Actions are important if you want to earn employees' trust and have interactions with them in the organization. Beginning from the leader, it takes involvement at every level to make a deep bond of trust that creates safety and motivates employees to put in the effort needed to make the organization successful.

Building Trust With People As A Leader

Leaders must earn trust the way everyone else does: by making a conscious effort to walk your talk, keeping your promises, and aligning your own behavior alongside your expectations of others. Once you cultivate that core, you'll constantly earn your team's trust. The most trusted leaders hold on to the fundamentals with trust-inducing behaviors.

The following are the most important ways a leader can build trust with the people:

- **Make yourself accessible:** Leaders should understand the importance of being approachable and accessible when building trusted leadership.

- **Be confident:** When leaders have confidence in themselves and their team, people trust them in return.

- **Be honest:** Simply telling the truth, even when it's difficult to do so, goes a long way in strengthening relationships and building trust. Don't sugarcoat your words, but also don't be heartless when delivering some tough love.

- **Show support for others:** When a leader shows support and encourages others even when they make mistakes, people will have faith in them. Understand what employees need and communicate it with them while considering their effort and being sensitive to their feelings. When you understand and support your team members, even when they make mistakes, it goes a long in building trust as a leader.

- **Be dependable:** People trust a leader they can always rely on for any issues they have.

- **Be consistent:** When a leader's words and actions match—not just sometimes or maybe most of the time but all the time—they've achieved a key pillar for building trust. Regularly doing what you say you will do will build more trust over time; it can't be what you do only once in a while. Keeping commitments must be an essential part of your behavior and relationships, day after day and year after year.

- **Be open:** When a leader actively listens, asks questions, encourages others to share their concerns then takes what others say into consideration, people trust that their voices are being heard. Actively listen and check for understanding by thinking over what you've heard. Use feedback tools to make sure everyone stands the chance of his or her voice being heard. You should engage in dialogue with employees, giving them the chance to ask questions, get answers, and voice concerns.

- **Show empathy:** Leaders should develop the skills to balance their team's needs and feelings. This attitude shows deep understanding and builds an equally deep trust.

- **Show gratitude:** Give credit when people do great work, and you'll set the stage for an appreciative culture.

- **Lead from within:** Leaders understand the importance of trust and take it seriously. They create a daily habit of keeping their words and actions trustworthy. Nothing speaks louder about leadership than a leader's actions, and the team's reactions are a more direct reflection of these actions than their team's level of trust.

- **Recognize that building trust takes diligence:** Trust must be earned over time. It comes from a conscious effort to steer your words, keep your promises and align your behavior together with your values. Building trust is well worth the effort because once trust is lost, it is often very difficult to recover.

- **Model the behavior you want:** Nothing speaks more loudly about an organization's culture than the leader's behavior, which impacts employee action and has the potential to drive their results. If you say, teamwork is vital, reinforce that purpose by collaborating across teams and functions.

- **Be accountable:** When you acknowledge their mistakes as successes, employees see you as credible and are more likely to follow your lead. You'll encourage honest dialogue and foster accountability by building processes that become a part of the culture. These include evaluating each project (positives, negatives, things to change) objectively, seeking candid feedback from all applicable sources, or holding firm to deadlines and milestones.

CHAPTER FOUR

THE THREAT FACTOR IN ORGANIZATIONS

Threats include anything that could affect an organization, like supply chain problems, shifts in market demands, or a shortage of employees. It is vital to anticipate threats and to take action to tackle them before you become a victim of them and your growth stalls. While leaders, for the most part, can't control external factors (market shifts, federal regulations, and the like) which impact their teams, they can choose how they respond to them.

Common Threats To An Organization

Threats are negative influences that can hamper the productivity of an organization and also give it a bad reputation. Here are a few.

Disengaged Employees

Unarguably, one of the most insidious threats faced by the organization is employee disengagement. Recent Gallup studies and workplace surveys show that as much as 67 percent of employees are disengaged at work. In fact, 85 percent of employees are either open to or actively looking at other job opportunities. This level of disengagement costs the U.S. economy between $450 and $500 billion annually. On an individual organization level, that equates to about $3,400 per year for every $10,000 spent in salary.

Talent Poaching and Knowledge Loss

A high rate of talent poaching is another big threat to an organization. When another company takes your talent, your organization then has to spend more resources finding and training a replacement. This not only affects the bottom line but the attitude with which a valued member leaves can have a dramatic effect on the culture that's left behind. Even employees who leave your organization on a positive note can be good publicity for new hires or remaining teammates. Make your organizational culture one where even those who leave to start a new life chapter want to take a piece of that with them and showcase it to others.

Safety and Security

Team members who don't feel safe coming to work are another threat to your organization. While physical safety is certainly a concern, I'm speaking of emotional and psychological safety. As previously mentioned in this book, trust is a powerful motivator and force multiplier in any organization. Trust is built when team members feel like they can be themselves at work, not as though they have to put on an act. With that trust, team members can focus on threats external to the organization, whether that be new regulations, a rival company, or an enemy military force. They know other team members have their back.

When that safety is nonexistent, team members are now fighting a battle on two fronts. One is against external threats while the other is against internal ones. Internal one typically wins out on where people focus as those tend to be more immediate in nature, more readily seen. Thus, members start looking out for "me" and not "we."

The Roles of Employees in Reducing Organizational Threats

Employees are the backbone of any organization. They play a vital part in controlling and reducing the threats to the organization. Leaders should strive to help individuals love their organization for them to deliver their best.

Respect The Organization:

The most important initiative to take towards reducing the threat to an organization is to genuinely develop a sense of respect for your organization. Don't love your organization simply because your boss has asked you to do so. The feeling must come from within you. The instant you are loyal towards your organization, your productivity would increase drastically, eventually benefitting the organization. Don't work only for your salary. In any case, money isn't everything; your career growth and professional goals are more important.

Be Loyal:

Commitment towards the organization is important. Blind loyalty for loyalty's sake has been the root of many crimes and strategic missteps throughout history. Instead, what I mean here is loyalty based on trust and values. Understand your organization's values and try to align yours with them. If you have questions about the directions or decisions being made and seem to not line up with company values, speak up and ask questions. This is easier said than done. Being "that person" comes with risks, but it's riskier devoting time and energy to culture and company that doesn't follow sound values.

Additionally, be willing and proactive in explaining decisions to your teams that your leadership makes. Understand what is being done at the higher levels and be ready to explain the thought processes to your teams. This may, in turn, generate questions from them that you didn't think to ask, which you can now funnel up as necessary. This fills the loyalty and trust meter your teams have for you.

Foster Open Communication:

I'm a firm believer that any topic can be discussed among teams as long as everyone agrees on a few simple ground rules.

1. Be respectful of all views, especially when you disagree with them.
2. Realize that no one has had the same life experiences or culture as everyone else. This will allow for a broader worldview when everyone is able to share their background.
3. Stay curious and ask questions of others with the intent to gain a deeper understanding, not judge or use the answers against them.
4. Know when to call "knock it off." Suppose a topic diverts into personal attacks, mocking, or topics whose comments may be considered illegal, unethical, or immoral by either company or team standards. In that case, it's time to call it quits.

Understanding Threats As A Leader

True leaders show courage in the face of threats and extreme situations. Effective leaders must also recognize the threats they face and the impacts they could have on their organization or personal growth.

1. Boundaries And Threats Are Not The Same
At the basics, threats are a knee-jerk reaction, a concept of "if you do this, it will result in this."On the other hand, boundaries are different; they are the extent to which each person can tolerate others in my space or in the spaces they manage. Once set, they are often enforced with a measure of dispassion that doesn't include the emotional charge of threats. For example, Hateful language isn't tolerated in a particular community collaboration space; hence any accounts using such language will have their post taken down, then be a warning, and then have their account suspended.

2. Threats Reflect APosition Of Powerlessness

Typically if an individual or entity issues a threat, they are actually displaying their fear and perceived powerlessness. There are several reasons people use threats. For instance, during a salary negotiation, for a raise or a promotion, you can say: "If you don't pay me more, then I'll have to consider leaving." This is a threat. However, it is better to say something like: "If you make me a good offer that reflects my position and worth and helps me to fulfill my very own needs, then it'll be greatly appreciated." Threatening to leave if your demands are not met is a fast way to undermining any remaining sense of shared purpose

3. Threats Can Affect Trust

Threats, although it reflects the information we see as true, always evoke the animal fight reaction. And they impact the trust in that relationship. You can repair this relationship somewhat, but it might never be back to an area of full trust. You can practice pausing before speaking and censoring any desire to utter threats when they brew up in your mind. Nobody wants to be in a relationship with anyone who threatens them, and neither do they have to.

Responding To Personal Threats As Leaders

If you have enough courage and influence enough people, someone somewhere could threaten you. Despite its certainty, you can mindfully brace yourselves for the moment it happens and emerge with your values intact.

1. Concentrate On Your Emotions

When we are faced with threats, we must first stop and concentrate. You can do a body scan through the app "Headspace." It's a good app if you don't regularly meditate. The analogy is this: Observe, with no judgment (only curiosity), the way different emotions show up in your body. For instance, when I'm feeling anxious or stressed, my chest becomes really tight. If I feel my chest become tight, I stop for a moment and concentrate.

Before you think that this is irrelevant stuff, let me assure you, one of the biggest factors to being an effective leader is self-reflection. Understanding what emotions you expose yourself to allows you to calmly react during a conversation or situation with a detached conviction that lends itself to powerful leadership.

2. Don't Interpret Feedback As A Threat

It has to be said that our instinct could interpret any feedback as a threat of "not good enough" and evoke an animalistic fear response as a real threat to our status or wellbeing. Listening to our own emotions helps us catch ourselves if our egos are running amok in this manner. We also need to understand this real threat for the sake of the people we lead and innovatively create situations where the feedback is more available to be incorporated and heard.

3. When Threatened, Follow Your Fear to its Logical End

When you feel threatened, the best thing to do is to follow your fear to its logical end. You have to move forward on this fearful course all the way to the end to discover the root cause of this fear. And, in facing the worst case, you'll discover that you are capable of facing that scenario and emerging on the victorious side; maybe not completely unscathed but definitely stronger.

Threats That Could Hinder Your SuccessAs A Leader

Being a successful leader in an organization doesn't necessarily shield you from career failure. The higher you go on the organizational ladder, the greater the danger of professional setbacks. Blind spots and mistakes at that level tend to negatively impact the organization at large, implicitly or explicitly, and by extension, yourself.

How can you handle a situation when you are headed for a fall? There are several threats that can stop you from becoming a successful leader if not properly managed. The following are some of the biggest threats to career success which I had encountered when I worked with emerging and established leaders, alongside strategies to overcome them:

1. The Lack of Self-Awareness

Leaders could lack self-awareness in two major areas: their impacts and their reputations. They are unaware of the way they affect others and of how people view them. A leader could pride in his ostensible ability to delegate, but his team could him as dumping tasks on them stupidly without matching the right tasks to the right people. They could also be bad at giving directions yet see themselves as giving their team complete freedom.

The most effective way to foster self-awareness is to actively ask for feedback. To encourage others to give honest feedback, especially direct reports from people who may fear retaliation. Leaders need to create a sense of psychological safety to foster honest feedback. For example, present your requests for feedback in a way that allows people to reply with a positive, forward-looking comment. Rather than asking, "What are the things that I should improve on?" say, "What do you think would make me even better as a leader?"

2. Not Learning New Things

Most leaders are busy. They are good at their specific jobs and highly task-oriented. If leaders are busy checking things off their to-do list, expanding their knowledge and capabilities beyond their current role could seem frivolous. Apart from being "too busy," however, those leaders could also have adopted a complacent attitude: "I've learned so much and have enough experience in my years here; I do not need to learn any new skill set."

But here's the problem: the world is constantly changing, with or without you. The tides are consistently changing. Your boss could also be replaced tomorrow, a round of restructuring may put you in unfamiliar territory, or the next technology may render your job obsolete entirely. By not thinking strategically about yourself in the big picture and not striving to find, learn and grow, you are endangering your career.

The antidote to career stagnation is a willingness to learn new things. Join a project outside your purview or deepen your knowledge of a strategic business area unrelated to your present responsibilities. For help, recruit mentors and subject-matter experts and skim widely from a spread of sources. Build relationships outside your current network and generously offer your expertise to others. Besides shielding you from career decline, these activities will yield a number of insights that will even take you up to the next level.

3. Bad Relationships

Not repairing difficult relationships can often be costly. Ignoring them can result in bad outcomes. There are only a handful of bridges you can burn before you find yourself isolated on an island of your own making.

Yes, this suggests networking, but it also means learning to manage and invest in better relationships with your boss or your employees, both of whom wield world power over your career trajectory.

Foster good relationships with everyone around you as well. If one or two people on your team have unconventional work approaches, talk to them about it. If you can't meet people on their own ground and learn various communication styles, your career as a leader will stall.

Furthermore, many rising executives neglect peer relationships. Having a negative reputation among your peers can hurt you, especially if you rise above them or they rise above you. If you didn't nurture those relationships, why would they feel the need to help you when they are in a position to? Be willing to assist other people without expecting anything reciprocally. Hone your networking skills, reach out to people in need, and be willing to have conversations. Not having time isn't a good excuse because managing relationships is simply as crucial to success as delivering results.

4. Not Delivering Results

Mastering office politics will definitely help your career, but you also need to deliver results. Business leaders are tapped for bigger opportunities precisely because they create value for the business, whether that's a rise in revenue, profit, market share, or a decrease in risk or cost. Ultimately, reliable performers usually get favorable attention from senior management.

You also need to be ready to communicate your results. Start thinking about your job not in terms of the work description but in terms of outcomes. What wouldn't happen if it weren't for you? What can you deliver reliably? How can you contribute to the larger vision and goals of the organization? Be ready to answer these questions very succinctly so you can deliver them in an introduction, in networking situations, with clients, and in meetings with senior leaders. Don't tell people your job title; tell them your purpose, the impact you have on the lives of others, and the way you impact the organization at large.

CHAPTER FIVE

THE PSYCHOLOGY OF LEADERSHIP

Leadership today is not about setting expectations and directing others to meet them. We recognize that we'd like to know our own and other people's natural tendencies, motivations and behavior, so we must create a culture that takes these under consideration and allows people to flourish.

This is why no matter how big or small your organization or team, leadership is the livewire of organizational survival; it can make or break your organization's success. It's been said that someone's experience of their manager accounts for at least 70% of the differences in employee engagement results. We have all heard the saying, people don't leave their jobs, they leave their managers, and the thing is, it's true.

This is the reality of our current world. Because the world of labor has changed around us, employees have begun to behave more and more like consumers; they go searching. Our employees would not just accept poor quality leadership anymore. You, me, them; our employees want more from their work, and if they aren't happy, they are going to leave. Perhaps you have already seen it in your own retention rates; probably, you have already moved on yourself.

In the development of the gig economy, people encouraging us to turn and to sample a variety of experiences and roles has paved the way for having good leaders who can provide our career needs and who we can give our loyalty and trust to. We all like to have a 'connected' leader.

A connected leader is a leader with high levels of self-awareness, someone who comes across as human, someone who isn't afraid to be vulnerable. A leader who is connected leader collaborates with their team and encourages honest dialogue and input from them reciprocally. A connected leader is a leader who will elevate people to be the best version of themselves.

The insight on leadership isn't all violets and roses, and it's all based on psychology and neuroscience research. Below is the psychology of leadership:

Trust Bonds: Trust is decided within seconds of meeting another person. This is often irrelevant to hierarchy and rank and is usually why having the ability to build a culture of trust is so vital for leaders today. Our brains are programmed to be highly aware, and in tune with our surroundings, and particularly the opposite person we share it with. When we meet someone, we plan to trust in the first few moments, and our bodies release the neurochemical oxytocin, which is related to social bonding.

After this chemical is released, it constantly increases the more we interact with that person. It then bonds us together and, at the same time, creates boundaries between those we are bonded to and people we are against. This suggests that if your team doesn't trust you, then you don't trust them as well, and this will eventually lead to a 'us' and 'them' situation.

As such, trust is key to being an efficient leader. If people don't trust you, you are fighting a lost battle. You can have a great vision, a good strategy, excellent communication skills, and innovative insight, but you just can't be an efficient leader if your team doesn't trust you. To build trust, you must ask questions, listen, and show gratitude.

Vulnerability And Weakness: Another of the psychology of leadership is a leader is showing that you are actually human. Authenticity and vulnerability are at the end of human connection. According to a social connection expert Brené Brown: "To make that connection to happen, we must allow ourselves to be seen, really seen." What is it that you neutralize your leadership that helps people (your team) ascertain what's important to you?

Too often, we lead from an edge of self-protection. We are concerned about our self-worth in the relationships we develop, and our fears of judgment, fear of disrespect, or "being found out" runs deep in us, even for leaders. Over and over again, we have been told that showing our human side – our vulnerability - is a weakness, but the truth is, it's not.

Vulnerability reflects a strength of character, a certainty in self and leadership, and it lets us lead by example, learning from our mistakes and paving the way for our employees to be human too. Vulnerability is a trait many leaders need to embrace. It can create deeper relationships and loyalty and enable people to bring their whole selves to the table. One of the biggest acts of any leader is to be publicly vulnerable to your employees and, by extension, to the world.

Positive Relationships And Positive Results

This statement might sound obvious. Leaders often fall back on the traditional command and control styles of management, in times of stress (or because they are aware there is no other way), usually result in anything but positive relationships.

When a leadership style doesn't foster positive relationships between managers and employees, the organization can struggle. Negative workplace cultures can easily fail to innovate or adapt to change. When people have a negative relationship with their leaders, they will most likely miss opportunities and stumble into more risk as nobody wants to speak out or act.

Research has revealed that positive relationships between employees and managers increase activity in areas of the brain related to openness to new ideas and social orientation towards others. Innovation and collaboration are two of the biggest quality of an efficient leader today.

Some of the top ranks for employee satisfaction are employee commitment and engagement. Positive relationships and connected leadership build an environment where people can connect with everyone around them, resulting in employees feeling more valued and understood better. Feeling understood and valued are two key factors in increasing employee engagement and commitment, helping to attract and retain top talent.

Becoming A Connected Leader

In today's world, work is not just about having a place to earn some money anymore. Most people have needs and need to have their needs met. They need a work they find meaningful; they need a desire, they need a purpose, and they want the work they will do to be valued. They need a job and a leader they can be connected to. So, in which ways can we increase how connected our employees are to us?

Simple things like checking out who they are in the real world, what their interests are, what they do at the weekend, and what truly motivates them could go a long way. Find out the challenges they face at work and home, help them sharpen their skills, or build their interests in a way that sparks joy for them. In short, treat them well—like people you want to stick around with for a long time.

Don't forget to show that you are human too. Show your vulnerability, ask for help when you need it, and build bonds with people up, down and each which way around you. Honesty breeds honesty. People with managers who are willing to ask for help when needed will build deeper, more connected relationships. These people will be better placed to tackle a challenge and handle more responsibility.

Effective Ways To Connect With People

Leadership is about people and relationships. Leaders don't just manage employees; they create sure employees are motivated, engaged, and inspired when coming to figure. Overlooking these principles may result in disengagement, loss of valuable employees, increased anxiety, and poor deciding, among others.

By not engaging with your employees, you'll miss out on key benefits that could contribute to you and your employees' success. Below are effective ways a leader can connect with people, create better relationships with your employees and increase engagement. By employing these strategies in your leadership approach, you will see a big difference in the way your employees interact and connect with you.

1. Stay True To Yourself

Staying true to yourself is exposing your best, worst, and true self. This is leading from your mind and your heart. You show up with: An openness to receive feedback, self-awareness of not only your feelings, emotional honesty, excellence in everything you are doing, a great attitude, and a grateful heart.

Employees want to understand what you have to say; they also want to understand what you represent. Staying true to yourself starts with self-awareness. You must understand yourself and be comfortable sharing who you are with your employees.

People do not follow leaders who they don't truly know and understand. You can't get anywhere with your team if they don't see you as a true person who is not perfect but has a real vision for themselves, others, and the organization at large. One key way to help people understand you is by staying true to yourself and connecting with others on a personal level.

2. Treat Others With Respect

Leaders make room for laughter and joy with others while accepting that they are not perfect and they make mistakes. These leaders will resist the urge to guard themselves at all costs. When they make mistakes, they openly admit them.

Anytime employees make mistakes, it's safe for them to admit it because of the high levels of respect and trust built over time.

3. Tackle Conflicts From All Sides

Leaders don't assume and jump to conclusions. They tackle difficult situations from different angles. They ask several people for perspective, get clarity, then determine a course of action.

Sometimes the ultimate decision might not be popular, but it is often the right one. You can hardly see a leader casting blame and pointing fingers. In handling conflict, leaders have the courage to focus on the storm because they know that cutting through a conflict to resolve an issue with respect and dignity is easier than facing the negative consequences of the conflict.

4. Speak The Truth

Don't sugarcoat things just to please others or to look good in front of others. Don't betray yourself or others by using false words or making decisions that don't align with who you are. Being truthful means speaking honestly and with integrity. That is why such leaders usually have great reputations.

5. Be Teachable

Another way of connecting with people is to be a learner. Leaders realize this will make them better. They know that everyone has something important to show them. The truth is that good leaders do not always know what's needed and what to do, and as a result, they are willing to ask questions and are sincerely interested in the answers.

6. Listen To Understand

Authentic leaders listen to understand, not to criticize or to judge. This is a rare and forgotten leadership skill. They do not dominate the conversation by talking about themselves alone or the task at hand. So in one-on-one discussions or meetings, they listen and reflect on what they've heard to gain clarity, and they ask questions to know the other person's feelings or opinions on the subject of conversation, which could be a statement as simple as: "Tell me how you feel about this."

Every time you are ahead of an employee, whether one-on-one or in a group, you have a chance to extend that engagement with dialogue. Compared to questions that give people limited options for response, open-ended questions encourage them to precise their opinions and concepts. Once you hear what they need to mention, showing interest and respect for their input shows you care, and therefore the impact is often significant.

To truly move employees to action, you have to understand what they care about and have a glimpse of their mindset. Stop talking too much. Ask for constructive feedback. People are a lot more likely to support what they helped to build. Stop talking at your employees and the monologues; have real, two-way conversations.

7. Be Accessible

Leaders who want to connect with people are always at the forefront of the organization, sharing plans for the long term, even during adversity when it's hard to see someone in the eye.

They don't cower behind closed doors or just delegate important communication to others. Employees usually look to leaders for information, clear expectations, and understanding of what is happening when the chips are down.

8. Value And Encourage Employees

Employees have to feel valued and inspired at work. You can consider scheduling several one-on-one discussions with managers, their team members, and individual employees. In more intimate personal conversations, managers can effectively address employees' concerns directly and offer them assurance that they are valued and have a future with the organization.

9. Recognize And Motivate Employees for Jobs Well Done

The best leaders know that the sole thanks to getting things done and move a business forward is through people. Meaning leaders need to transcend lifting employees who need extra motivation and recognize those that exhibit behaviors you would like to still see. Saying many thanks for employment well done and rewarding employees who exhibit your required behaviors seems simple, but it's often overlooked.

9. Be A Model For Others

Be aware that employees hear what you say, and pay close attention to what you do. The truth is that when it comes to keeping employees engaged, action communication comes first, and sometimes it speaks louder than words. Reflect on what others see in you and develop the ability to play the role of the leader you would like to be and to model the actions and characteristics that you would really like to see in others.

10. Embrace Conflict

Having tough conversations and communicating difficult issues is a component of a leader's job. The principle I share with leaders who avoid conflict is that they should embrace the conflict. Like the popular saying, sometimes, you have to go to war to achieve peace. When a conflict is handled well, it could lead to improved relationships and trust.

CHAPTER SIX

THE ART OF LISTENING

Listening is one of the most vital skills a leader should have. There are several other skills that define a leader. However, listening could be a difficult skill to master because it requires us to be more attentive, engaged, present, versatile, and open. Good listening skills in this digital era, thanks to information overload and shortened attention span, are fast becoming a rare attribute. Listening involves paying adequate attention and making nonverbal cues in regard to what is being said.

Many people are guilty of starting a conversation and putting an idea or question on the table. Still, we don't give ourselves the opportunity to concentrate on what others have to say as we never stop talking, or we are so focused on formulating our reply to what we assume they will say. Don't just listen with the external ear but with the internal ear. Listen with the intention of understanding.

Listening is the inspiration for excellent relationships. This is because it shows that you care. Empathy and listening go together; you cannot display empathy or effectiveness if you are not listener. The standard of our listening determines the standard of our influence. Employees want to be heard and respected. Listening transmits that type of respect and builds trust. This results in more motivated and committed team members.

On average, we retain just twenty-five percent of what we hear, which is due to our business and lack of listening skills. What is your chatting talking to the listening ratio? Listening is crucial to have a complete understanding of situations. Without full understanding, you can easily waste everyone's time solving the wrong problem or merely addressing a status, not the basic cause.

The greater your success, the more you have to remain in-tuned with fresh opinions and perspectives and welcome honest feedback. Listening is the best way to realize your team goals and create a successful strategy. The truth is that well-informed decisions steer the organization in the right direction because good leaders are active listeners.

It's no secret that knowledge and wisdom aren't gained by talking but by listening. Listening is an art that includes taking note of that "still small inner voice." If something is wrong, just don't attempt to justify it. Although you can escape with it for a time, eventually, the price must be paid. Having true integrity starts with mastering the art of listening.

As a leader, your job is to encourage others around you to be open and honest without negative consequences. Listening results in personal awareness and growth. If you are not a listener, you'll not grow. In addition, be open-minded when employees offer their ideas and differing opinions.

Poor communication comes with a high price. It accounts for businesses losing plenty of revenue annually. For organizations to remain strong in this competitive market, their leaders must understand the need to embrace change and continually improve. Leaders have to master the art of "Lead with Listening." The success of your organization could be dependent .on it

Becoming A Better Leader Through Listening

When employees say they need their voices to be heard, they are actually saying they need leaders who won't just hear them but really hear them. As employees look for more attention, feedback, and support, leaders have become more mindful of personal needs in order to more effectively stimulate professional growth and overall performance. Leaders who listen build trustworthy relationships which are transparent and breed loyalty. You can recognize the leaders who have their employees' best interests at heart because they really hear them.

As a leader, it's difficult to actually know what your employees are thinking about, what's troubling them, or the way to help them get out of a performance slump –unless you are actively listening to them. Listening transcends being quiet and giving someone your full attention. It requires you to remember visual communication, facial expressions, mood, and natural behavioral tendencies. Listening should be a full-time art when you consider the uncertainty embedded in the workplace and the changes happening.

Leaders must balance their intensity and desire to perform with compassionate attention to their employees' needs. Being more mindful of the employees' stress and their tension points before they affect the business demands that we up our effectiveness.

Listening is a leadership responsibility that doesn't appear in a leadership description. Those who listen to their employees are in a far better position to steer the increasingly multigenerational and diverse workforce. The "one-approach-fits-all" method of thinking has become outdated, and people who embrace the art of listening are destined to be the higher, more compassionate leaders.

The following are some listening strategies you can employ to help you become a better leader:

Show that you care

When you care about your employees, they have the tendency to work harder and aim to exceed your expectations. Employees want to be led by those that genuinely care about them and what they represent to the team and organization at large. Don't just see your employees as resources or tools to build your own success, but as people and valuable gifts who bring unique capabilities and ideas not necessarily restricted to their job functions.

Several leaders have said that their employee-employer with their staffs' relationships end at work. These types of relationships are usually short-lived. Employees want leaders who truly care about their general well-being and are reliable in times of professional and private hardships.

Engage yourself

Aside from caring, be engaged in issues paramount to your employees. Whenever they share their opinions, ask questions and encourage them to elaborate and expand on their perspectives. Whenever you engage yourself more actively, hold yourself accountable, and follow up with your employees, they will know that you are actively listening and listening and trying to know what matters most to them.

A boss once told his employee that he had only a single way of expressing himself in meetings. Rather than trying to mold him into being someone he wasn't, he embraced his style and learned to use it to help enhance their team meetings. Repeatedly he asked him to lead meetings when he was unavailable for it. He made him feel that he was listening because he valued and applied what he interpreted about his style into action. To the present day, this employee is extremely grateful for having such a compassionate leader as a boss – as he gave him the additional incentive to be his authentic self.

Show empathy

The workplace is filled with the strain and pressure of every day. Because all employees tackle stress and pressure in different ways, it is vital that you are empathetic to how these things impact your employees' performance. Show your concern and let your employees know that you feel their frustrations. If you are an old-school leader, do not be afraid to show empathy even if you feel that it'll weaken your stature or authority as a leader.

Empathy is a powerful display of listening. I have realized that a lot of leaders avoid emotional interactions, but the best leaders empathize and make themselves accessible to those that need attention.

Don't judge

This was touched on a bit earlier, but leaders that judge others are not listening to leaders. Too often, leaders make harsh criticisms about those with a special style or approach. Rather than judging someone, you can learn from them. When leaders judge, they show their immaturity and inability to embrace differences.

These leaders may enjoy a long period of success in a company, but they often find it difficult to recreate the success when they move to another organization. Leaders must be complacent; they must embrace new ideas and strategies. They need to be more active listeners, constantly learning and adapting to different views.

Be keenly mindful

Good leaders are extremely mindful of their surroundings. They actively seek information beyond the apparent verbal and non-verbal communication. They acknowledge others through visual communication, facial expressions, and nods. These types of leaders possess an incredible degree of executive presence and are tuned in to the dynamics of things happening around them at all times.

Leaders who are mindful aren't just listening to conversations; they take note of them and engage in the dialogue. They don't fake it; they listen to what is being said and how it is being said. As a leader, people are constantly watching all your moves and action. If you appear disconnected, you'll be perceived as disinterested and not listening. Never stop being mindful.

Never Interrupt

Has your leader ever rudely interrupted you while talking? It's fair to say this is often a standard occurrence. Compassionate leaders are listeners who do not interrupt the flow of the dialogue. They welcome two-way communication and are aware that each interruption results in disengagement. They earn respect from people by being a patient listener.

Be focused on what your employees are saying. Be in the moment and be respectful to others. Listen and become a more compassionate leader. Employees respect leaders who listen.

The Process of Active Listening

Many other sources touch on the importance of active listening, but I think it bears repeating the high points here. Our world today is filled with plenty of distractions. With the constant rise of media and technology, many people have lost our ability to actively listen and sometimes find comfort within the screen of our phone. However, suppose we will retrain ourselves to specialize at this moment and truly hear our people. In that case, many issues within the workplace are often avoided, and you'll get to understand your people and better understand their needs so as to form them happier.

The listening process is usually divided into five distinct stages, which are: receiving, understanding, remembering, evaluating, and responding. This is often the most ordinarily mentioned model when analyzing good communication because it helps isolate the required skills required at each step.

Receiving The Message

This is the first and basic stage of the listening process, the act of truly absorbing the message being expressed to you, whether verbally or nonverbally. Not all communication is completed through speech, and not all listening is completed with ears. No matter how you are communicating with another person, the key at this stage is to concentrate.

Understanding The Message

This is the next stage in the listening process, and it's the stage where you plan your response. Understanding takes place after receiving the message from the person sharing and starting to process its meaning.

You can understand by asking open questions or rephrasing parts of what the person shares with you during the conversation. This enables you to demonstrate your active engagement with their words and helps you better understand their key points.

Remembering What Was Said

What's the essence of a conversation if you forgot everything the person had just said? This stage of the listening process might sound almost like the first two, but it transcends merely absorbing and processing information. Remembering entails retaining that information, and the best way to do so is to identify the key elements of a message. This can be done using the following methods:

- **Identify the small points:** By converting a set of small details into a topic, you'll be able to turn something potentially complicated into an easy-to-grasp general concept. The small points will remain in your memory and help you understand them better and remember them longer.

- **Familiarize the message:** Relate the main idea to something you already know. This should be easy to do as there aren't many new ideas out there, and the likelihood is that the discussion you are having will bring back old memories and past experiences. Use this to help you retain incoming information.

Evaluating The Message
This is the stage, you start to organize your response, but remember: You are still a listener, not a speaker. When the message has been absorbed, processed, and remembered, you can start to evaluate the message in parts.

Responding To The Message
If you are done the receiving, understanding, remembering, and evaluating stages of the listening process, responding should be easier than ever. You'll be prepared to deal with the person's most vital points, with an awareness of the circumstances and context surrounding their words.

CHAPTER SEVEN

PERSONAL CARE TO BE AN EFFECTIVE LEADERSHIP

By far, the greatest concentration of research in leadership has been applied to the area of effective leadership. An easy demonstration of the importance of effectiveness in leadership is a simple question. When you consider a "perfect leader," what comes to mind?

Most people would consider someone who has the entire trust of her staff, listens to her team, is approachable, stays cool under pressure, and always makes careful, informed decisions. They would naturally describe an effective leader. However, if the question was, "How would you describe your current boss, supervisor, or leader?" no doubt the responses would vary greatly.

Leadership and management styles fluctuate significantly, and different styles may be more appropriate in different scenarios but below are what separates effective leaders from other leaders.

How Effective leaders Differs From Others

1. Ability To Focus

Effective leaders are often recognizable by their ability to focus. Effective leaders do not generally recognize multitasking as effective or productive. Rather they focus on one thing at a time in their pursuit of a goal. This is not to say that they do not have multiple competing priorities. Rather, they recognize the importance of devoting their attention singularly to a defined amount of time to ensure focus and organized success. The idea of multitasking as it has traditionally been understood is being shown consistently in recent studies to be ineffective, if not outright mythical.

Highly effective leaders can see the value of focusing on the task at hand and organize their schedules accordingly. Whether spending time with children, or a spouse or working on a project, they are able to tune into that moment and experience it fully. They also are self-aware and tuned in when their focus is waning so that they take steps to remain with their commitment.

It is worthy to point out that some people have a higher capacity to focus than others. In many cases, there are physical challenges that make focus particularly difficult. Some of these can be overcome with additional effort; others may require medical or medicinal intervention. A leader can recognize and admit their difficulties and seek the appropriate assistance. This is part of being self-aware.

Apart from medical matters that may contribute to difficulties in focus, there are many recommended actions that have been shown to improve this area and make us better able to focus and be more effective. The following are some of the things that could enhance your ability to focus:

Exercise regularly: A study published in the British Medical Journal confirms the numerous benefits of regular exercising. In respect to the study, a short 10 to 40-minute period of exercise resulted in an improvement in mental concentration and focus. This means that even a quick walk can have major benefits on your focus, productivity, and general well-being. If you intend to achieve a focused mindset, regular exercise is something within your control that you can easily implement.

Have a healthy schedule: This involves organizing your tasks and activities in a way that gives you sufficient time to complete each one without hindering the other. When you have a healthy schedule, your quality of sleep enhances too. Having a routine that includes a regular sleep schedule contributes greatly to energy and focus. Those who sleep better are generally quicker thinkers, have more focus and concentration and retain the mental and physical energy to maintain high levels of focus and lead effectively.

Organize your workspace: A disorganized workspace is a known cause of undue stress and creates distractions and time delays. An average person loses an hour a day to disorganization. Whether or not you are particularly accustomed to the mess inhabiting your life, clutter will still have a noticeable effect on your concentration. An effective leader takes the time to consider the effect that disorganization may have on their time and effectiveness and recognizes the value of the organization for improved focus and success.

Take a break: Sometimes, the best plan is to stop – just for a short time. Taking short breaks will help improve your ability to maintain focus over long periods of time. If you find yourself unable to remain focused, then you should definitely give yourself a break. Short mental breaks will refresh you and help you to stay focused on your tasks. It is important here to ensure that we do not let our breaks become a haven for procrastination. Effective leaders recognize when their focus is being challenged and look for ways to recharge or reset, such as short breaks throughout the day.

Schedule Due Dates/Times: Assigning time and deadlines for which you have to complete a task will enhance your ability to focus on completing it. This will help you keep distractions aside and make realistic decisions about what you can accomplish within the timeframe that you have scheduled.

2. They are Driven By Purpose

The first of the habits that distinguish effective leaders from many others is purpose orientation. Effective leaders are generally in the habit of setting realistic, clearly defined goals and living according to a stated purpose. This is a part of effective leadership that involves preparation and intentionality rather than waiting on things to happen and reacting to them.

To this end, effective leaders spend time considering their purpose and associated goals. This applies to their professional purpose as well as their personal one. They will consider the one-year, five-year, ten-year plan. What is their role, and what goals must be reached to realize the plan? They may even have a personal written mission statement. Thinking in this way empowers leaders to think in "big picture" ways that help them remain grounded when smaller things go awry.

In order to have a plan, there must be a goal. In order to have a goal, there must be a "why." The "why" is the purpose. A purpose can be as specific as "meet this deadline" or as general as "Always be committed and truthful and empower and equip others for success." A purpose may (and likely will) change as circumstances change or as the leader grows in responsibility or understanding. What is important is that, as an effective leader, you devote time to considering your purpose in order to formulate your plan and what you are driven to achieve.

Some self-discovery questions may be helpful. What are you good at doing? What are the gifts and talents you have? In what areas are you least effective? Most effective? Where would you like to be five years from now? How would your staff describe you now? How would you like for them to describe you? What values do you want people to see in you? Effective leaders are built from self-discovery and purpose. Find an effective leader, and you'll find someone who is clear on their purpose, is driven, and has a plan.

Many leaders fail because they pursued more money or a title and became overwhelmed. They did not plan well; they did not pursue their purpose; they were not effective in their decision-making. An effective leader is better able to consider if a move is right for them if they can be effective, rather than being driven by excitement, money, or power.

Effectiveness typically comes with satisfaction and self-fulfillment, and satisfaction and fulfillment generally come along with good choices made by leaders who know their purpose.

3. They Are Action-Oriented

While thinking before you speaking or reacting is a trademark of a leader, so is being poised for action. The problem of "analysis paralysis" is a rare thing indeed with the effective leader whose bias for action is delayed only by his desire to act appropriately.

It is important to organize, plan, and set priorities, but a plan is no more than a potential without action. This is what distinguishes effective leaders from those who are less skilled in EI. Effective leaders act quickly, often, and when necessary, not allowing fear or anxiety to cloud their judgment.

Effective leaders do not wait for the conditions to be absolutely perfect before they take action; they do not procrastinate. On the contrary, an effective leader will seek the most positive and productive activities that can be taken, and then the next, and so on. The action may be adjusted with new information, but the bias for action is steady. This is not to say that he is overly hasty, only that he is efficient with his considerations for the facts available and looking for an opportunity to move as soon as it is right to do so.

On the other hand, procrastination is the enemy of effective leadership as it implies that the needed action is known but just not begun. This is often the result of fear or anxiety, or indecisiveness, or simple lethargy. A person who procrastinates is either succumbing to overwhelming emotions or simply isn't an action-oriented leader.

If you are prone to procrastinating and want to build your effectiveness and penchant for action, the first step is to recognize this in yourself and then commit to improving in some key areas. Here are some things to consider to move toward action-oriented, effective leadership.

Be Organized: There are a lot of tools that help with organization. You can get a paper planner or work schedule. You can use digital devices with planning tools and apps with set reminders. You can also schedule regular meetings to keep status up to date on a given project or task.

Personally, I like to use Trello (the free version) to organize by task, not time. I've noticed over my professional career that when people organize their day or week on a time basis, tasks will expand to fill a given amount of time. This tends to be true even if the task is not very complex or complicated. For some reason, we feel the need to fill every minute of our day. Therefore, I organize my Trello board with "To Do," "Time-Sensitive," "Working This Week," and "Three Personal Weekly Goals" lists. At the beginning of every Monday morning senior leadership meeting, I create cards with tasks and place them in the respective lists. As I complete a task, I remove the card from the list by the end of the day. The key, though, is that I do NOT create new cards after the weekly stand-up meeting. I prioritize what I need to work on, sit down to focus on the task, complete it, and then move on.

Now, you may ask yourself how I handle the ever-present email inbox taskers. The answer is quite simple. I dedicate two hours per day to answering emails. The first hour starts shortly after I arrive at the office, and the last hour is right after lunch. Ingraining this habit of not obsessively checking emails as they come in is an ongoing battle, but certainly worth it. I have more time to get away from my office and around to my teams for all manner of chit-chat, mentoring, learning, or coaching.

Oh, and I highly encourage my teams to do the same.

Break Your Goals Down Into Simple Achievable Tasks: One of the reasons why we procrastinate is because the needed action looks too big and overwhelming. We don't know where to start. While it is largely viewed as pertinent, and typically is what an effective leader would do, to tackle the largest item first, a different approach is often effective to build momentum when combating procrastination. Schedule smaller tasks working toward the larger one. For example, a project to plan the office Christmas party can be broken down and delegated to others to call caterers, get bids for food, reserve the venue, schedule entertainment, create invitations to save the date, etc.

If you break them down into simple enough parts, you will find that they become more easily achievable and provide quicker evidence of progress and small victories to celebrate. As you become more effective, however, you will find the "top-down" approach valuable, starting the most difficult task and rolling downhill from there.

Eliminate Distractions: Before you start a project, eliminate all potential distractions that might hinder you from meeting deadlines or cause you to procrastinate. Typical distractions that lead to procrastination – or just take our attention away from the more important task are phone calls, emails, and other communication platforms, which draw our attention and prevent focus. If you struggle with procrastination or are easily distracted, you might consider scheduling time away from your devices to work on the project. You can also use the "do not disturb" settings if available and turn off your phone for a designated time. Additionally, you can simply make others aware that you are working on a project and need not be disturbed for a particular period.

It may be that you have personal distractions as well that should be addressed, such as television, radio, internet, social media, etc. The effective leader knows herself and what she can and cannot allow in her space when the focus is needed.

Involve Others: It is more difficult to procrastinate once you've brought in additional people and the expectations and accountability that come with them. Share your objectives with people close to you, such as your partner, friends, colleagues, and family. Tell them the things you intend to achieve and how you intend to achieve them. When possible and appropriate, involve others in your projects who can help to keep things moving and hold you to the agreed-upon timeline. You will find it easier to motivate yourself when you are also accountable to others.

4. Effective Leaders Have A Positive Mindset

Having a positive mindset is not a result of being effective; it is the. Effective leaders do not entertain negativity but rather recognize the difficulty of a given situation. They generally believe that there is a way through or out of every challenge. This habit of maintaining a positive mindset even in the face of negativity has made effective leaders more effective and more sought after for their input.

In your quest to become an effective leader, you will encounter many challenges that may make you question yourself and your abilities. If you do not have a strong positive mindset, you will often give up even before the real difficulties present themselves. A positive mindset enables you to see the potential in everything.

A positive mindset is created as a result of a positive inner dialogue. An effective leader presumes there is a way to succeed even if he cannot yet see it. A positive mindset is invaluable to our development as leaders and goes a long way in determining how we see ourselves and how effective and successful we can be. People who do not have a positive mindset or have low self-esteem and self-confidence often doubt themselves and begin to operate from a position of protection from failure rather than one that assumes success. From this perspective, leaders cannot be consistently effective as they would rather not accept the project to avoid failure than taking on the challenge and find a way through. When you find yourself regularly doubting yourself, believing you lack the capacity or ability to get a task done, having a potentially paralyzing fear of failure, then you have a negative mindset, and you most likely struggle to be an effective leader. When not properly and promptly recognized and managed, a negative mindset can rob us of opportunities to grow and succeed.

Here are some ways to exercise effectively and to keep your mindset in check, and work toward maintaining a positive one.

Be aware of your emotions, mindset, and thoughts: This is the first step to achieving a positive mindset. It may seem simple, but this self-awareness is pivotal as, without being aware of your thoughts and emotions, you can have no control over them. You can see a negative mindset coming from far off once you learn to practice keen self-awareness and resolve to push toward a positive mindset. Devote time to self-awareness learning what triggers your negative emotions so that you can be prepared to counter this response when the opportunity arises. This is effective in action.

Learn self-acceptance and self-compassion: This is not the same as accepting where or who you are, as if it is all you will ever be. On the contrary, it is simply accepting that you, like everyone else, have a starting point from which to launch your journey to better effect. It is foolish to believe that change will come overnight. Give yourself a little praise and celebrate the small steps. Give yourself permission to fail along the way, but refuse to accept failure as the final destination.

Take action to control your thoughts: Once you've practiced awareness and allowed yourself the opportunity to learn from your mistakes, now you can take action. Did you know that you are capable of thinking something else? Of course, you may not fully control what comes to your mind, but you can change the script. For example, a negative mindset might assume that if a co-worker is not with you, they don't like you.

A good response using a positive mindset might stop this thought process and consider other possibilities. It very well may not be you at all, but simply an unknown factor causing the co-worker to behave this way. So, you may not stop the negative thought, but you effectively un-think it through a positive mindset. You own your thoughts and actions, so should any negative thoughts creep in, you can banish them immediately and replace them with positivity.

Minimize the influence of negative people: Surround yourself with people who motivate, trust and inspire you--and, in turn, are inspired by you. In your quest to cultivate a positive mindset, you have to realize that you must limit your exposure, when possible, to negative-minded people. Being overexposed to people who have a negative mindset will not only reduce your chances of becoming a positive-minded person, it can also drain you of the support and energy you need to exercise a positive mindset. As a leader, you cannot avoid such people entirely, but you can minimize your interactions and their impact on you.

5. Freely Ask For Help

This habit is simple but not always as easy for many to cultivate. Those in leadership can often feel that asking for help is a sign of weakness. However, the effective leader is self-aware and recognizes her limitations and is not afraid to ask questions or request assistance when appropriate.

In addition to recognizing their limitations, effective leaders recognize the importance of viewing things from other people's points of view and their own as well. They respect the views of others and seek to understand why they see things the way they do. Hence, they do not hesitate to seek help to broaden their knowledge and enhance their effectiveness and productivity as well.

The habit of refusing or being reluctant to ask for help is one of the single biggest habits that prevent people from becoming effective. Truthfully, not asking for help may provide short-term comfort; but this is usually at the expense of long-term development. As it is impossible for anyone to know more than they know, it stands to reason that seeking input from others would be a good way to get answers to questions and better ourselves and become more effective and genuine leaders.

6. Effective Leaders Have Integrity

Integrity, matching your words and actions and seeking to do what is right in all circumstances is essential to be an effective and effective leader. For an effective leader, integrity is equally about being true and accountable to yourself, recognizing your own struggles and shortcomings and taking action to overcome them. It could mean not taking on a project when you are "overbooked" or including others with skill sets you will need to be successful.

Integrity is not a fleeting or relative concept but a steadfast adherence to a strict moral, ethical code; being completely honest with yourself, with others, and in your actions. Integrity promotes openness, empowers us and others, demonstrates consistency, commands respect, and allows for increased clarity of purpose and action. Integrity, in fact, promotes higher effectiveness in people. When you live an honest life, you become more conscious of your decisions and their consequences, the way you talk, your feelings, the thoughts you have, and the actions you take.

When others begin to recognize our integrity, trust soon follows. With greater trust comes greater effectiveness and greater respect and credibility.

7. Leaders Are Proactive

In addition to developing effective as a leader with a responsibility to your organization, you are also given charge over a group of people, many of whom look to you for behavior modeling. There are some practical strategies to help you become effective as a leader:

1. **Anticipate problems:** Use your empathy to understand your employees and how they interrelate and determine what motivates them. The more you recognize how your employees feel, the fewer surprises you are likely to encounter. You will be able to "smell" the storm in the air before it arrives.

2. **Communicate often:** Few things are more startling emotionally than receiving bad news for the first time at an official review. Create a safe space for regular discussion, which allows you to head off any emotional "bombs" by addressing concerns early with time to make corrections. Once employees are accustomed to a boss who is concerned about their needs and speaks with them regularly, your effectiveness will begin to be contagious; they will be less anxious and more open to feedback.

3. **Support personal and career growth:** Offer your time to help employees get where they want to go. As an effective leader, you are familiar with the confidence that comes from having a plan. Help your employees develop one and build in supporting tasks/steps to attain it. If they see themselves elsewhere, make a deal with them. You'll help them get there so long as they continue to commit to the mission where they are in the meantime. This partnership approach is indicative of an effective leader.

4. **Don't Over-Commit:** In order to maintain your integrity as an effective leader, it is important to be aware of scheduling and commitments before promising any special attention to the staff. It is a damage to trust to have to cancel meetings or be unable to follow through on a promise. It can be a challenging balance to be present with employees and remain dedicated to the other requirements of your role. But with some good communication, clear boundaries, and you're effective, you are equipped for it.

5. **Create flexibility and adaptability:** Rigidity is often assumed by employees, and flexibility is often viewed as a vulnerability by young or undeveloped leaders. However, as an effective

leader, you understand the influence that empowering employees to succeed can have on their own EI development. Create an environment where their ideas and best practices can be shared and considered.

6. **Create a culture that inspires others to be effective:** Just like any other skill, effective needs time and constant practice. Therefore, leaders should create a culture where employees can practice and execute their effectiveness. Ensure that employees know what it is and how to enhance it. (ahem, see next chapter) Assure your employees that your organization cares for them.

7. **Set goals that promote effectiveness:** Actively work to extend effectiveness among your workforce. Have them read a good book, something like; the Effective Key maybe. Then set some goals with them to create a space for growth. Below are some samples of what these goals could look like:

8. Identify your emotional triggers and discuss them together with your teammates. Once a month, attend lunch with a co-worker whom you don't know well. Show a willingness to be more accessible by asking a team member for feedback on a project. Spend one week without using any negative remark-get creative.

CHAPTER EIGHT

COACHING AND MENTORING

Coaching and mentoring have the same primary purpose: helping others grow, develop and reach their full potential. Both methods give people the chance to meet their responsibility for their own personal and career development.

The two are frequently categorized as one when discussing people development. Still, there are plenty of differences between coaching and mentoring, so it is vital to address them as separate things and understand how they can work together.

Coaching Vs. Mentoring

Mentoring is sharing knowledge, skills, and experience to help another develop and grow, while coaching provides guidance to a person on their goals to help them reach their full potential.

One of the most distinct differences between these two terms is that mentoring is directive, while coaching being non-directive. What does that mean in practice? Well, in mentoring meetings, a mentor is most likely to do more of the talking, whereas, in coaching, the coach asks questions and gives the person they are coaching the opportunity to reflect and do a large aspect of the talking. Ultimately, both coaching and mentoring are about helping people to get to where they need to be by leveraging the experience of the coach or mentor.

The Differences Between Mentoring and Coaching

Below are some of the key differences between mentoring and coaching

S/N	Mentoring	Coaching
1.	Mentoring is usually long-term, with some mentoring relationships lasting over six months, and in many cases, mentoring can last for years or even decades. In fact,	Coaching is usually short-term and could be as short as a fast ten or fifteen minutes conversation. That said, some coaching relationships are often long-term too.

	many famous mentors and mentees say they have lifelong mentoring relationships.	
2.	No qualifications are required for mentoring, which suggests that it's easy for organizations to start out mentoring programs quickly. Yes, mentoring training is usually recommended, but it certainly isn't required, and actually, there are only a few mentoring qualifications offered compared to coaching qualifications.	Training is needed in coaching skills, and lots of coaching qualifications are available and nearly always necessary and positively recommended to be a very effective coach.
3.	As said earlier, mentoring is a lot more directive. It's about the mentor sharing their knowledge, experience and skills, discussing with the mentee and guiding them in the right direction.	Unlike mentoring, coaching is non-directive, which suggests that it's about asking the right questions, providing the opportunity, confidence, and trust for the individual being coached to think about how they will achieve more, attain their objectives and find capabilities within themselves.
4.	Typically, mentoring is a little less structured than coaching, and while having a mentoring meeting and goals are suggested, it'll be up to the mentee to piece this together, compared to coaching, which usually follows a more rigorous structure.	Usually, coaching is structured by line managers or sponsors, so organizations will often send an employee for coaching, or a line manager will sponsor an employee to be coached with new skills.
5.	Finally, mentoring is development-driven and leaves the mentee to make a decision about what they want to achieve and which goals they need for his or her mentoring relationships.	Coaching is typically performance-driven and encourages those being coached to perform in their day-to-day roles.

The Key Elements of Mentoring

Mentoring Is Long term

Mentoring relationships usually have the potential to last a lifetime if they end in friendship. Although you initially get a mentor to support you with a specific goal, you can reach out to them again in the future when you have that reference to someone. Mentoring tends to be in the long run than coaching partnerships, thanks to its personal and informal nature.

Mentoring Is Voluntary

Mentoring is usually voluntary. Either the mentoring happens informally through personal networks, or formally through an organization mentoring program, there's hardly an expectation of financial payment for the mentor's time. Both parties are focused on the mentee's personal development, and the process is also highly rewarding for the mentor. Mentoring succeeds because mentors wish to 'give back and know that mentoring is beneficial for them as well.

Mentors see their jobs as more meaningful and less stressful than those that don't mentor, and they have also had more chances of getting a promotion.

Mentors Offer Advice And Guidance

The role of a mentor is to focus, learn, and advise. It's about directing their mentee in the right way and enhancing their career development. The primary distinction between mentoring and coaching in this aspect is that mentoring is a softer and more relationship-focused type of guidance, as against a coaching's structured training approach.

The Mentee Drives TheMentoring Sessions

In mentoring, the mentee is tasked with driving the sessions and leading the relationships. A common misconception is that a mentor has to tell you exactly what to do and mold you into a successful person, but the opposite is actually the truth. The mentee needs to be dedicated to their own development and utilize their mentor to help them achieve their goals.

The Mentor Gives Advises Based on Personal Experience

As a result of the personal nature of mentoring, a mentor usually draws on their personal experiences and expertise to give advice to their mentee. This could be done through sharing a story that taught them a valuable lesson or a challenge they overcame in their career. This type of personal dialogue is welcomed and encouraged in a mentoring relationship.

The Key Elements of Coaching

Short term

Coaching relationships are more short-term than mentoring relationships, thanks to the very fact that they are objective-driven and more structured. Someone may need a coach to help them develop a specific skill or run through a specific limiting belief. The coaching usually ends once that skill or objective had been achieved.

Training and Skills Impartation

As against advising and guiding, coaching focuses more on training and skill impartation to help you develop a success mindset. A coach can help build your self-awareness: identifying areas that need improvement and challenging assumptions that can prevent you from achieving your goals. Coaching is usually used to hone leadership skills, where you'll be trained in the art of challenging yourself to manage others better or identifying limiting beliefs in yourself.

A Coach Allows the Coached to Drive the Session

Unlike in sports, where a coach takes the lead in training and developing those under their purview, in the form of coaching discussed here, the coached takes the lead in affecting change. The coach is the sounding board, mirror, and facilitator through the tough bits.

When team members come to you with a problem, the goal of a coach is to allow the member to walk through a situation and keep them focused on solving a problem. Coaches need to not jump to a solution, although every good leader definitely wants to be a problem solver. By helping the member stay on track and discover the root cause as well as solutions themselves, they are more likely to feel empowered and capable of solving future problems on their own. I like to think that a coach's job in this context is to work themselves out of a job.

On that note, I'd really recommend a book called *The Coaching Habit* by Michael Bungay Stanier. There's a wealth of knowledge and practical steps to follow for the aspiring coach.

A coach doesn't necessarily discuss personal experience

A coach isn't obligated to discuss anything personal. In fact, there is a high chance they have no experience in the industry or role that their client works in. This is often a key difference between coaching and mentoring, where mentors would draw on their experience and knowledge to offer advice.

Similarities Between Coaching And Mentoring

In both mentoring and training, there is:

- Sharing of knowledge
- Development of skills
- Focus on career progression
- Unlocking of potentials
- Development of self-awareness
- Discussion of goals
- Trust between both parties
- A desire to develop
- Exposure to new ways of thinking

The Skills Required for Mentoring

For mentoring, while qualifications aren't required, there are many skills that are recommended for somebody to be an efficient mentor. Here are some of these skills:

- A keen interest in helping others.
- First-hand experience, insights, and knowledge in the area in which you are providing mentoring. Mentoring is built on concrete and solid advice and guidance.
- Interpersonal skills and relationship building are crucial for mentoring.
- Dedicated long-term time commitment. While this is not potentially considered a 'skill.' It is vital because if you start a mentoring journey with someone, it's important to see it to through to the end.
- Motivating, encouraging, and galvanizing energy throughout all mentoring meetings.
- Helping to spot the mentee's goals is crucial. This will take some self-reflection from the mentor so as to help the mentee and tell them where their goals should be.

The Skills Required for Coaching

A relationship between a coach and coached is of mutual affection and respect, and this is vital to a successful coaching relationship. The ability to maximize resources and encourage the coached is similar to that of mentoring. The following are some of the skills required for coaching:

- The ability to identify strengths and challenge the individual being coached so as to take them forward.
- The ability to stay curious about the situation enough to ask questions that force the coached to think.
- Ability to raise awareness and responsibility both with the individual being coached and at an overall office and organizational environmental level.
- The skill to be real and find the right balance of interpersonal skills and the practical skills to convert discussions into actions.

The Key Benefits Of Mentoring and Coaching

Both mentoring and training have a wide range of advantages, which, when used correctly, can benefit both the individual receiving mentoring and coaching and the mentor or coach and the organization too. Here are some benefits of mentoring and coaching:

1. They are extremely effective learning techniques.
2. They are often formal and informal, with mentoring often seen more informally and coaching often sees more formally.
3. They can increase employee engagement and retention when applied.
4. They are easy to implement into any organization or business structure, and increasingly we're seeing organizations running both.
5. They can increase confidence and the interpersonal skills of the person providing the mentoring or coaching and the person receiving it.
6. They can drastically improve individual performance.

CHAPTER NINE

THE NEGATIVES OF MICROMANAGING

Micromanagement, in simple terms, can be defined as a style of management in which a manager closely monitors or controls the activities and work of subordinates or employees. Micromanagement usually has a negative connotation because most people see it as management's attempt at digging its fingers deep into the business of those actually doing the work.

So why do leaders micromanage? Leaders micromanage because it is a way for management to ensure that tasks are performed in a very precise manner—in other words, in the management's way. The problem is, it isn't always the right or most efficient way of doing things. And that's only one of the risks of micromanagement.

You know what level of supervision to give an employee can be difficult. If you provide insufficient oversight and guidance, people could find themselves feeling lost, unsupported, and unproductive. On the other hand, if you provide an excessive amount of supervision, you'll find yourself micromanaging your team, which usually makes people resentful and resistant.

The Effects of Micromanaging on Employees

Anyone who has been micromanaged knows it's no fun, but it can affect everyone. Some employees will do their best to earn the trust they desire when they are being denied. While this might sound beneficial initially, it can have damaging long-term effects because they typically blow out of proportion when that trust never comes.

Others can become hooked into micromanagement and won't risk making a move without approval. They have no initiative due to fear of being reprimanded, which leaves them ill-equipped to handle change and adapt to changes. These employees don't grow over time because they have no incentive to enhance their skills or demonstrate their expertise.

Another category of employees reacts negatively to signs of micromanagement. They resist, argue, push back, and usually make an unpleasant show at every opportunity. While being micromanaged is often an incredibly unpleasant experience, these employees often become so bound up in expressing their displeasure that their performance suffers because of that. The very act of striving to make them productive then ends up achieving the exact opposite.

Why Leaders Micromanage

In most cases, micromanagers are driven by the desire to regulate situations and be in charge of other people's work because they think productivity will be of poor quality. Other explanations for micromanaging might include:

- The assignment is huge, and that they can't afford any mistakes.
- They don't trust someone to do things correctly.
- They want the work done to be 100%.
- They consider their way of doing things the best.
- They see someone struggling, and that they want to help them.

The Problems With Micromanaging

If the purpose of micromanaging is ensuring success for the organization, what then is the problem with micromanaging, and why should it be stopped? There are several reasons why micromanaging is often damaging to an organization, and they include:

Loss of Control

When employees are micromanaged, you restrict yourself by the management tools you have at your disposal. And, one funny thing about control is that when it's your only means of management, you always find yourself losing it. You lose control and time when you try to micromanage your team. It is vital to understand that there are many valid management styles, and each employee reacts differently to each.

Loss of Trust

Micromanagement will eventually result in a huge breakdown of trust between you and your staff. Your staff will not see you as a manager but a despot whose only desire is to frustrate his staff. This crushing act destroys what little trust is left between employee and employer. When trust is broken, two things can happen a significant decline in productivity and loss of employees. Although the latter is a worst-case scenario, it still happens.

It Builds Dependent Employees

When micromanaged, your employees will become dependent upon you instead of having the confidence to perform tasks on their own. Micromanagement makes your team need your constant guidance. Dependent employees take time and energy to manage, which may take a toll on your schedule and energy. You need to know that those employees were initially hired because they offered something unique to the organization: skills, talents, and insights, all unique to each employee. When your employees aren't dependent on you, they will think on their own—and when employees have the liberty to think on their own, great things can happen.

If you micromanage, your employees' skills, insights, and talents can fall to the wayside, leaving you with a team that only knows how to do what they are told. I'm sure you want to give your employees the liberty to think and act on their own.

Results in personal Burnout

Micromanaging is downright exhausting. Looking over numerous shoulders a day will burn you out very quickly. Eventually, you'll end up hating your job, straight down to the very organization that employs you. If you hate it enough, you'll even find yourself leaving it and possibly never eager to take on a management role again.

Sure, burnout is usually a risk in any job, but the energy burned while micromanaging will ignite that burnout faster than anything. This sense of burnout can affect not only your work life but can stretch into your home life and cause anxiety and depression. And don't forget that burnout can affect those beneath you. Managers aren't the only victims of burnout; as you burn out, you'll very likely take your staff with you.

Micromanagement isn't only bad for your employees, but it can take a terrible toll on your physical and psychological state. Take time to step back, breathe, and acknowledge that your team can handle its tasks without you constantly hovering over their shoulders.

Mass Exodus Of Staffs

Simply put, most people don't take kindly to being micromanaged. When employees are micromanaged, they usually do one thing; quit. Considering the explanations why managers micromanage (ego, insecurity, inexperience, perfectionism, arrogance), It's simply not worth the high employee exodus. Having to always train and retrain staff not only robs you of momentum, but it also makes your organization lose the skilled and effective employees it once had for second hands and under-qualified people, which then affects the orbottganizationandruins morale. Friendships are made and ruined, and eventually, this may crush the spirit of your staff.

Lack of Independence
When employees are micromanaged, they begin to feel as if they have lost their freedom. When this occurs, they will gradually lose the will to do anything but that which you demand. Nobody will step outside the box or go the extra mile for a task. Lack of autonomy will impair growth in your employees, and one of the goals of management should be to help employees rise through the ranks.

No Innovation
One of the most common dangers of micromanaging is ruining your employees' creative spirit. Your team is in charge of leading your project, and that they know what is happening better than anyone else, including you. While some innovations won't break through, crushing innovation and creativity destroy all chances of the great ideas beginning and being shared. By declining to take risks in innovation, you are also declining the opportunity for progress.

Why Micromanaging Your Employees Is Harmful

A predictable response from a micromanager could be that they are concerned about an employee making mistakes. While this might seem justifiable, it's important to know that making mistakes is one of the most effective ways for an employee to grow. Working in the face of failure also helps to build resilience, which is incredibly important in today's fast-changing world. In addition to developing assessments that identify which skills an employee must work on, making mistakes is critical to professional growth.

But what if they make plenty of mistakes? The truth is, that's actually not a bad thing. If an employee regularly fails to meet targets, it is a good indication that they have to be reassigned to another role or stepped down altogether. An excessive amount of micromanaging often allows subpar performers to scale unnoticed by the organization, which hides the team's deficiencies.

There are many instances where managers may have to play a more active role in an employee's work, but that doesn't necessarily mean they are micromanaging. Some of these instances include:

Training new employees: Even someone with extensive experience will need guidance and support while learning how things are done at another organization.

High-stakes projects: Know the distinction between project management and micromanaging your employees. A project which has potential legal ramifications or high financial stakes should have regular supervision and audits to ensure that it is on track and all stakeholders know the project's current status.

Correcting performance issues: If an employee consistently did not meet expectations, they will need to be monitored or placed on a performance improvement program. However, these efforts are aimed at assisting the employee in arriving at a point where they will meet expectations on their own.

How to Stop Micromanaging

Everything boils down to trust. You trusted your employee enough to hire them. If your training is top-notch and your instructions are clear, there's no reason why you shouldn't even be ready to trust that employee to be accountable. This is often very true of organizations that used various cognitive and behavioral employee assessments throughout the hiring stages to make sure they are making the best selections possible.

It is often scary to step back and let people try and possibly fail, so start gradually. Identify the smallest bits of important processes, assign them, delegate, and walk away. Relate people's skills to the risks of the assignment at hand. An unskilled employee who is given a high-risk task should be closely managed. Alternatively, a project of such magnitude should probably be assigned to a more seasoned employee in the first place.

Understanding the way to identify and avoid micromanaging your employees is critically important for all leaders. Even when the micromanager seems to have the employee's best interests at heart, there are only a few situations where micromanaging your employees doesn't result in negative outcomes of some kind. Organizations can only achieve success when everyone embraces trust and accountability, which ensures that employees can specialize in doing their own jobs to the best of their ability without unnecessary oversight or support.

If you find yourself micromanaging, you need to fix it immediately. You need to have that trust and faith in the people who work for you and believe that they will get the work done even without your constant oversight. With more freedom, they will eventually surprise you with a rise in innovation, productivity, and creativity.

CHAPTER TEN

WORKPLACE CULTURE

What Is Workplace Culture?

Workplace culture is defined as the collection of attitudes, beliefs and behaviors that structure the regular atmosphere in a work environment.

Whichever way we define it, workplace culture is usually tricky to navigate. It is how it feels to be at work instead of a group of written rules. All organizations have a personality and atmosphere – and that's not something easy to adhere to.

In the era of notable changes to working life, organizations are awakening to the very fact that you can have the best strategy and the best people in the world, but it doesn't matter if your culture isn't right. Culture is the very air you breathe. If it's toxic, your organization dies.

The Importance Of Workplace Culture

That's why the attention on culture is the biggest priority for organizations looking to rework how people work - and the way they feel about work. Here are some specific reasons it is so important, the areas it can impact, and how you can affect positive changes to your organization's workplace culture.

1. Employee wellbeing

Does your organization value psychological health as much as physical health? Workplace culture has a key impact on employees' wellbeing. Well-being was voted as the top trend of importance in the 2021 Deloitte Global Human Capital Trends study. A whopping 80% of leaders said it is essential to their organization's success.

Many organizations have embraced remote working and installed measures to offer their employees a far better work-life balance, including flexible work hours based around childcare. This will help the employees feel supported and valued.

2. Employee performance and productivity

Workplace culture has an impact on the way people perform, which, ultimately, can directly impact your organization. A happy and supportive workplace energizes the employees to work optimally every day and enhances mood and concentration. Organizations that have stronger cultures are generally more successful and have high productivity levels. According to research by Oxford University, happy workers are 13% more productive than unhappy ones.

3. Communication

Effective communication helps to create mutual respect and trust, no matter the individual roles and responsibilities. Workplace cultures where people can't ask questions, pitch ideas or easily connect with one another are less transparent and won't bring out the best from people. But in what way does that change when you encourage an open and two-way conversation?

If you create a more open working environment, employees feel empowered to speak in constructive ways. Brainstorming sessions and meetings become more valuable as organizations hear real opinions and fresh ideas from every corner of the business. And ultimately, that's good for business.

4. Recruitment

Organizations with robust workplace culture and brand identity are more likely to draw in the right talents. Having a website that clearly defines your organization's core values and objectives makes it easier for job candidates to determine up whether they would be a good fit for your organization. It's also an opportunity to convince top talent that your values and your culture are the right fit for them.

5. Engagement and retention

Positive workplace culture is one that values its employees and their contribution to the success of the business. Employees who feel they are a part of a community instead of a cog in a wheel are more likely to remain with an organization. Companies with healthy cultures are several times more likely to retain their employees. This not only results in long-term loyalty but also cuts the costs involved in continually having to recruit new talent.

6. Teamwork

The most successful organizational cultures comprise of people from all backgrounds and nurture a way of solidarity. Even people who have very different outlooks and personalities can gel if they have a good purpose to support. The very best performing teams are increasingly insisting that diversity of all types is critical for fulfillment.

Thriving collaborative workplace culture can break boundaries between teams. On the other side, a toxic environment can make employees selfish and develop a blame culture.

7. Quality of services

A positive workplace culture inspires employees to strive for the best quality in what they do. It is easier to bring the most out of individuals who feel comfortable at work and are empowered to make decisions. This builds a high-performance culture that strengthens the entire organization and helps to make sure products and services meet the very best standards.

8. Reputation

You might have seen posts about organizations on social media sites giving them a bad reputation. Many of those come from ex-employees. Employees judge organizations based on their interactions with them, and a negative image can do plenty of damage. Businesses with a robust social conscience who follow ethical working practices and support staff wellbeing tend to have a better reputation.

Having a good reputation can have a hugely positive effect on business, but a toxic culture has the potential to do the exact opposite. Over time, an environment where employees dread getting to work and don't have their supervisors support them can bring an organization to its knees.

9. Morale boosting

Culture and morale are intrinsically linked. Like culture, employee morale isn't always a simple thing to pin down; it's a mixture of engagement, attitude and mood. But you will always know for sure when it's low. Building a positive culture that focuses on wellbeing and inclusion can help build morale by making each employee feel heard and valued.

Healthy workplace culture is a core component of building team morale by allowing teams to feel confident and empowered in what work they do while encouraging individuals to be themselves and voice their valuable opinions.

Building Workplace Culture

Building an excellent workplace culture doesn't happen overnight. It evolves and changes with every interaction about work. But, to get started, try the following key strategies:

1. Organizational values

It's crucial to have clear core values that truly reflect the philosophies and beliefs of your organization. Employees need to realize and invest in these, so ensure you are communicating them effectively.

Make your values real. Do not just sit on a sheet of paper and ask yourself what your values should be. Start by watching the things your organization does. How do you treat employees and customers? How active are you in the organization? How diverse is your leadership team? These answers are going to be indicative of your real values.

If you think that something is missing, add it as an aspiration and decide to change behaviors to align with it. Likewise, if you discover that your organization's values aren't what you want them to be, decide and take action to change them.

Whichever way you go about it, your values should be reflected in your actions or be a part of a transparent transformation strategy to mark your behavior. Otherwise, they are just words on paper, and your employees will quickly realize that.

2. Organization identity

Your identity is what the organization is and ensures it stands out from the rest. It's important because your identity is the way people inside and outside the organization perceive you. Maintaining a positive identity is important if you want to demonstrate your organization's professionalism and social responsibility.

3. Leadership

The way leaders and managers communicate and the way they encourage teamwork and openness is crucial to creating a healthy feeling in the workplace. According to a study, six out of ten people said their manager is the reason they left their organizations. It is clear that lack of trust is hampering relationships. That is why leaders should find ways to specialize in coaching or developing and empowering their employees to do great work instead of micro-managing.

4. Employees

Your employees are your greatest asset, and a various pool of talent can bring different personalities, skills, beliefs, experiences, and values into the mix. That's something to be celebrated. An organization culture where everyone is comfortable and included will help the employees unleash their full potentials at work.

Look beyond sexual orientation, race, and gender to nurture everyone as a person. With only 32% of employees feeling truly like themselves at work and only 44% of employees saying their company's diversity and inclusion strategy feels sincere, there's a huge opportunity for organizations to enhance their workplace culture.

5. Workplace norms

Workplace norms are the rules and traditions which guide how people do things. They are not usually written down. And they are often so embedded that people can become unaware of behaviors and actions, even though they are inappropriate. This is because they've become ingrained in everyday routines; they help create a sense of normality. But simply because an organization has always done something a particular way doesn't mean it's acceptable. As workplace norms evolve, everyone must understand the way they should conduct themselves at work.

6. Policies

Organization rules, policies, and decisions and can all shape organizational culture. Recruitment, onboarding, training, performance management, dress codes, recognition programs, wellbeing and work-life balance can make a difference to the success of your organization. Most especially, having a clear, transparent policy for bullying or harassment shows you are taking inappropriate behavior seriously.

7. Communication

With the rapid rise of remote working and dispersed workplaces, open communication is critical for productive workplace cultures. Employees must remember they need to remain in line and know what's happening in their organization, even if it doesn't affect them directly. They need to access information quickly, collaborate, share ideas and solve problems wherever they are and at any time.

All teams can have interpersonal conflicts from time to time, but a healthy work culture will help you resolve issues quickly and professionally.

8. Working environment

A working environment is a place where everyone feels safe, engaged, inspired, and productive. Your workplace's physical setting is vital because it impacts how people carry out their duties day in, day out. Noise levels, temperature, lighting, and desk arrangements can all affect mood, whether working in an office, warehouse or home. Nobody wants to feel uncomfortable while they are working.

9. Subcultures

If you are working for the same organization, you are all on the same side, right? Not necessarily. A 'them vs. us' situation can usually build up between distinct teams or departments if there is no effective communication.

Subcultures in your organization have the capacity to disrupt the general culture. But positive subcultures that complement one another can get everyone working together to realize the same overall aims and objectives.

Characteristics of a Healthy Work Culture

- Employees are cordial with one another. They respect their colleagues and bosses. Backbiting is taken into account as strictly unprofessional and is avoided for healthy work culture. One derives nothing out of conflicts and dirty politics at work.

- Each employee is treated equally. Partiality results in demotivated employees and eventually an unhealthy workplace culture. Employees must be judged only by their work. Personal relationships have to take a backseat at the workplace. Don't favor anyone simply because he's your relative or friend.

- Appreciating the best performers is vital. Praise them and encourage them; allow them to feel indispensable to the organization. Don't criticize those who haven't performed well, instead ask them to work harder next time. Give them another opportunity instead of firing them immediately.

- Encourage discussions at the workplace. Employees must discuss issues among themselves to succeed. Everyone should be allowed to freely express their views. The team leaders and managers should interact with the subordinates frequently. Transparency is essential at all levels for better relationships between employees and healthy workplace culture. Data tampering and information manipulating is a strict no-no at the workplace.

- Organizations should have employee-friendly policies and practical rules. Asking an employee to work till late into the night on his birthday is just impractical. Rules and regulations should be made to profit the workers. Employees should maintain the decorum of the organization. Discipline is vital at the workplace.

- Leaders should be more like mentors to the workers. The team leaders should be a source of inspiration for the subordinates. The superiors are expected to provide direction to the workers and guide them whenever needed. The team members should have access to their boss.

- Promote team-building activities to bind the workers together. Conduct training programs, workshops, seminars and presentations to upgrade the current skills of the workers. Prepare them for the tough times. They should be ready under any odd circumstances or change in the work culture.

How Workplace Culture Starts With The Leadership

Building a workplace culture requires participation from everybody within the organization, but it must start with leadership. The general vision, the company policies, and the day-to-day practices must all align to create a cultural transformation or maybe to take care of the type of culture you currently have.

Leading a culture transformation is not a small task, which is why many organizations are reluctant to undertake it. However, with a transparent vision, an idea to execute it, and a robust commitment, leaders can change the minds and hearts of the people who make the organization.

Workplace culture is the sum of the behaviors of all the people in an organization. While every individual plays a role within the culture, leaders have to wield the most influence because they set the vision, formulate company policies, and set an example for workers. For these reasons, defining the type of workplace culture you want requires intentional effort on the part of the leadership. Knowing and understanding how leaders influence others around them is critical if you create a particular workplace culture.

Leadership Sets the Vision
The leader is responsible for defining the organization's vision and ensuring that others in the

organization both know it and embrace it. The company vision plays a role in culture because it influences the choices that are made. For instance, an organization that desires to remain on the leading edge of its industry must be world-class in innovation. In the same vein, an organization that wants to provide the best customer experience must have the people and processes to be completely customer-centric.

By defining the vision and sharing it with the organization, and demonstrating the expected behaviors, leadership sets the pace and would always link actions and behaviors to the vision; either they support it or don't.

Leadership Creates Policy

An organization's policies should support both the vision and the desired culture. For instance, an organization that prides itself on being family-friendly must have policies to support this claim. Otherwise, the words fall through, and the vision never comes to fruition. Even worse, policies that counter the mission and culture can negatively affect morale and reduce the credibility of leadership.

When undergoing a culture transformation, know-how your existing policies do or do not support the specified culture and change them accordingly. In addition, know the policies that don't exist yet and what changes you need to make to sell the culture you are trying to create. For instance, if the corporate mission includes supporting the organization's community, a policy that has paid days off for volunteer work would encourage employees to plan to partake in such activities.

Leadership Models Behavior

When building a workplace culture, it doesn't matter what leaders say; what matters is what they do. For instance, if you are trying to create a workplace culture of productivity and line managers aren't working productively, don't be surprised when the workers they supervise imitate them. On the opposite hand, a manager that stays late to help complete a project will encourage team members to display an equivalent level of commitment to their tasks.

Leaders at every level must display the kinds of behaviors you are want to implement in the workplace culture. If leaders don't model the specified behavior, employees won't take the culture transformation seriously and can still operate in the usual way. On the opposite hand, when employees see changes happening and the positive effects of these efforts, they will be motivated to participate as well.

CHAPTER ELEVEN

THE IMPORTANCE OF 360-degree FEEDBACKS

Good communication is a key component of each successful organization. In order to make the team operate at their peak efficiency, crushing their goals and dealing collaboratively with each other, it's important to continuously gather regular feedback from everyone in your organization.

Sometimes this will be a stressful or uncomfortable process, but it doesn't need to be! Mostly, when done correctly, 360-degree feedback is always both rewarding and beneficial for everybody involved.

Good 360-degree feedback is a consistent format that involves pre-selected, carefully thought out questions that aim to give everyone in the organization an opportunity to be heard and provides proper feedback. Everyone has the chance to share the good things they see in the team's work and voice their concerns or means in areas that would help improvement.

In addition to receiving feedback from others, participants even have the chance to perform a self-assessment. They use this to ascertain how their own ratings are compared to how others assess their competencies, which results in greater self-awareness and opportunities to grow.

When most people are involved, each individual has the chance to get clear feedback from multiple angles, allowing them to adopt a growth mindset and become the simplest they will be.

What Is 360-degree Feedback?

360-degree feedback is the process by which feedback is generated by the people working with and around an organization. The feedback is usually confidential and always anonymous. This feedback involves all the people that the individual interacts with regularly. This includes his or her managers, supervisors, peers, and therefore the people that report back to the individual, also the people to whom the individual reports to.

A mixture of individuals drawn from the above categories will be asked to fill out an anonymous feedback form. The form will contain several questions associated with various aspects of labor and other workplace competencies. There also can be rating questions and questions that demand a descriptive answer. The individual who will receive the feedback also will be asked to self-assess and refill an identical feedback form.

360-degree feedback is not just for the workers of the organization but also the management and, therefore, the leaders. Lately, it's generally performed online due to the simplicity and convenience offered by 360 appraisal software.

Why 360-Degree Feedback is Vital For Leaders

At first, we fully believe that the strength of each company is in the employees. Our main focus is on helping each individual in an organization become the best they can be, and in doing so, it helps the entire organization. However, most organizations have a manager-employee structure, and lots of professionals currently believe the managers to spot and provide feedback on strengths and growth opportunities.

The reality is that anyone can be a leader in an organization, and hopefully, that leadership isn't harmonized into managerial roles. One of the simplest ways to develop leadership is to provide 360-degree feedback to everyone and to develop a growth mindset in each individual. In addition to the above benefits for individual professionals and teams, there are additional benefits for managers, or more appropriately, the leaders in organizations.

1. Share the Responsibility of Feedback

Company leaders are already caught up with numerous responsibilities that make it difficult for them to offer their teams the time they have to help them grow. In this way, 360-degree feedback allows teams to require more responsibility for themselves and apply their own leadership and collaboration skills to assist their team in becoming more efficient and productive. It's also a good way for leaders to remain in tune with their teams through the regular gathering of feedback and to get feedback on their leadership themselves.

2. Create an organizational Culture Built on Communication and a Growth Mindset

In every organization, the leaders set the manner for the way the organization thinks, acts, and behaves. The best teams create an organizational culture that's built on communication, and therefore the continuous effort to grow and improve.

As a leader, implementing and managing a 360-degree feedback program can help shape the organization's culture to make a strong growth mindset. Not only can leaders lead by example, sharing the items they're working on and allowing the team to give feedback on them, but it also gets the whole team into the habit of respectfully sharing ideas without the fear of offending or overstepping.

3. Demonstrate Accountability

One of the most important roles of any leader in an organization is to make their team responsible and be in charge of their quality of labor. When a 360-degree feedback routine has been implemented, leaders have the chance to remain accountable to their teams on an endless basis and reciprocate that expectation with team members. Combined with a growth mindset, a practice of accountability drives growth and efficiency within the team and organization.

How to Implement a 360-Degree Feedback Program

While any 360-degree feedback is positive for an organization, there are definitely some best practices that will assist you in getting the highest value from your feedback routine. 360-degree feedback should give a chance for growth and support, and proper procedures and organizations are required to making sure that this is often the case.

1. Discuss the Importance of Feedback With your Team

The only way any 360-degree feedback routine will work is that if your whole team is bought in. A mutual reason why feedback is required and the way a daily feedback system provides great opportunities for self-awareness and growth is completely vital to the success of such a routine.

Discussing the necessity for feedback and presenting the thought of how to remain during a growth mindset and support one another in your personal and career growth helps the organization achieve goals and get everyone on the same page. At now, you, on the other hand, may have the chance to resolve concerns and objections upfront, rather than running into them later down the road.

Once the team has agreed that a daily feedback routine would be a positive practice for everybody, you'll begin to organize your programs in the appropriate way for your team.

2. Choose Feedback Timing

An effective 360-degree feedback routine operates on a frequent and continuous basis, but it should also allow time for effort and growth in between. This might look different between organizations or maybe between teams within the same organization. Some teams may decide that shorter feedback practiced more frequently is perfect, while others might spend a much longer time with a more robust feedback practice less frequently. This could be discussed and recommended within the team.

3. Decide How Feedback are going to be gathered

When it involves sharing feedback within a team, especially when there are sensitive topics to debate on, it is important to make use of a procedure that helps each team member feel safe and support both the feedback they share and the feedback they receive.

Because feedback comes from everyone around each team member, pulling everyone into an interview setting can take much of your time and make the team members only communicate directly with a supervisor or designated leader. If this is often recommended because it is the best way to gather and share feedback, then this is often a completely reasonable method.

Many companies have found that gathering feedback is often much simpler when employing a tool or platform like Matter that manages the method for them. Matter features a ton of built-in features that make the management of 360-degree feedback that creates gathering and receiving feedback easier than ever.

Automatically request for feedback on your agreed-upon timeframe. Each team member gets reminded to provide feedback at an acceptable time but can provide that feedback when they're available instead of interrupting or taking an excessive amount of time of their day.

Request feedback from anyone, not just the people in your organization. Easily request feedback from everyone you're working with, including your team, partners, clients, customers, and vendors.

Focus on specific areas by choosing a skill to work on. Adjust feedback inquiries to develop in those areas, allowing you to trace your progress over time.

Work towards specific goals with goal-setting tools. This will measure your progress whenever you receive feedback, so you'll really dive in and ascertain where you would like to work on. Keep your feedback documented, so you'll always ask for important advice and tips and track your performance and growth.

The Benefits of 360-degree Feedbacks

360-degree feedback can have a good range of advantages, as discussed below, divided into appropriate categories.

For Teams

1. Improvement in Communication: For teams, communication is significant, and 360-degree assessments enhance it considerably by giving each member the chance to voice his or her feedback.

2. Enhancing Synergy: By providing feedback, members begin to know each other better, resulting in improved collaboration. They begin functioning more in unity. Team synergy is improved as their goals and processes are aligned.

3. Improved Effectiveness: 360-degree evaluations allow each member of the team to know the extent and quality of contribution he or she is making to the team. They will work on any problems being faced by the organization to become the best members of the team.

For Individuals

1. Boost in Self-Awareness: This is often one of the most fundamental benefits that 360-degree feedback provides to individuals. The reports and reviews provided by the feedback highlight the areas in which they will improve on, also as their existing strengths. Individuals become more conscious of themselves and their role within the organization.

2. Discovering Strengths: This is essential for the individual strengths to be recognized and acknowledged allowing him or her the opportunity for personal improvement. Recognition of strengths allows a development decision to be made for every individual.

3. Accurate Overview: Since the feedback is gathered from multiple sources at different levels, it provides a more accurate idea about the individual's behavior, performance, and capabilities.

4. Discovering Blind spots: Individuals can discover and understand the behaviors that they exhibit without them noticing. Proper steps can then be taken to beat these blind spots.

5. Skill Development:360-degree feedback gives each individual thought of the talents that they have to work on or that which they lack. A development plan is usually made for every individual's improvement.

For Leaders

1. Multiple Perspectives: Leaders are originally easy in getting good or zero feedback from their juniors. However, the anonymity of 360 feedbacks allows the feedback to be good. In addition, a more comprehensive report is generated since individuals from different levels are going to be providing the feedback.

2. Encourages Evaluations: The most important advantage of 360-degree feedback is that an environment of learning and improvement is often created. Employees are going to be inspired once they see leaders actively participating in the feedback and implementing the required changes.

CHAPTER TWELVE

EMPLOYEE BUILDING AND DEVELOPMENT

For most organizations, employee building and development is about making their employees better employees. However, employee building and development goes beyond making employees better employees; it entails making employees better employees and better people as well.

Making employees better people involves planning growth based on their values and goals and aligning those values with organizational goals to create buy-in/ownership from every team member. In addition, tasks are designed to play to a person's strengths but with enough difference and challenge and grow them.

Knowing how to make everyone on a team a far better person is usually so frustrating and challenging. But it is usually easy if leaders have a basic understanding of human behavior, what makes people tick. Therefore, leaders must have the knowledge of what truly inspires employees to be better people.

Below are some strategies to help you motivate your employees to be better people:

1. Start with scheduling

Get off on the right track by developing clear goals and expectations an operational reality. You are doing that through the lost art of one-on-one conversations, which is an excellent motivational tool. Leaders thrive once they strengthen relationships with their people by spending more one-on-one time with them to listen to their suggestions, ideas, problems and issues also as talking about performance issues and their work. But first, you would like to understand the way to structure these meetings so that it works to your advantage.

2. Determine what motivates them

Do you know what gets your team members out of bed in the morning? What they're hooked unto, their goals, aspirations, and interests? In other words, does one really know your team members? Great leaders show an interest in their people's jobs and career aspirations so as to motivate them the proper way. Once that has been established, they emerge into the longer term of making learning and development opportunities for his or her team members. They determine what motivates their best team members by getting to know what desires will drive each team member. This is often about emotional engagement.

3. Provide the resources they have to try to do their work exceptionally well

It's a simple question, but you would be surprised how often it's not asked: What does one need immediately to try to do your job better? You may be surprised, or maybe shocked at the answer; it might be that they have access to more information to make the proper decisions, better equipment or maybe another workspace. Working on what you discover is going to be an enormous motivational booster.

4. Praise and compliment them often

"I do not like to be recognized," said nobody, ever. Leaders need to get into the habit of praising and complimenting their members for their good qualities and work. The businesses in Gallup's study, with the very best engagement levels, use recognition and praise as a strong motivator. They found out that employees who receive praises on a daily basis increase their individual productivity, receive higher loyalty and satisfaction scores from customers, and are more likely to remain with their organization. How regular are we talking?

5. Help co-create purposeful work

People want meaning and purpose in their work. When people find purpose in their work, it improves that person's happiness and boosts productivity. A method to offer employees that purpose is to allow them to meet the very people they're helping and serving, even though only for a couple of minutes. Managers giving their people access to customers in order that they can see firsthand the human impact their work makes is that the greatest human motivator.

6. Help them develop new skills

Although important, I'm not talking about putting them through another required technical or safety training program to keep them or the business compliant, but actually giving them meaningful new skills or knowledge in other areas that they will use to improve their natural strengths for future roles, whether with their current company or another company. The purpose is to serve and value them as exceptionally well as people and workers that they need no reason to go away but use their newfound skills for brand new projects.

7. Actively involve them.

Great managers recognize that leadership doesn't mean a method but is multi-directional. While it can come from the highest down at critical times, the simplest scenario is allowing decisions, information, and delegation to travel from peer to peer or from rock bottom-up, where the collective wisdom and involvement of the entire team help solve real issues in real-time on the frontlines.

8. Believe them.

The best managers often delegate and provide their employees' responsibility for delivering challenging work. If this does not happen in your workplace, consider two hard questions:

Do you trust your knowledgeable workers to try to do what they have been hired to do?
Do they need the proper competence for the work to hold out the work with confidence?

So often, managers underestimate the potential and skill of their employees to use their brains! If you answered yes to the questions above, be of the mindset to always accept that they will do the work. Then, give them the space to perform and support them with whatever you have to make them even better. This is usually how you motivate them to do the tasks.

9. Invest in personal development

Your employees don't just exist in a professional capacity to serve your organization. Their whole employees are comprised of physical, intellectual, and emotional experiences. For them to evolve both personally and professionally, employee development must be holistic. This includes:

Emotional balance
Ask questions like, "How do you feel about your work lately? Are you battling anything? This means our basic emotional needs must be seen, heard, acknowledged, and validate, needs that always go unmet in many work environments.

Intellectual growth
Books and seminars don't just need to be about business. You can provide continuing training around personal finance or fostering healthy relationships.

Physical health
Encouraging your people to step far away from their desks when the workday is over and allowing them to practice more self-care shows that you simply don't just depend upon the talents on their description, but you care about them as people.

When employees are given the tools to do their jobs well and train to advance in their careers, they're more likely to feel inspired to try to do their best work. And your reputation for stellar employee development might just encourage the simplest and brightest candidates to hitch your team.

Apply individual strengths to realize the team's overall goals.
Help your team understand each other's strengths and the way these talents unite to make a strong picture and improve teamwork skills. Speak to the strengths of individual team members in the presence of project compatriots. Suggest how the team might cash in on others' strengths and hear what the team has to say. Look beyond your projects to the broader organization to ascertain whether demonstrated strengths are often utilized in neglected areas of the broader business.

3. Assign team projects that support employees' strengths.

You would never intentionally assign tasks supporting weaknesses, but you would possibly overlook strengths unless they've surfaced.

4. Incorporate strengths into performance conversations and reviews.

Help employees set goals supporting their core competencies and strengths. But also be mindful of challenging them in areas where they can grow. The mistake many leaders (and people in general) make is that they want to shore up the areas in which they are weakest. These forces focus away from continued growth in developing strengths. Instead, leaders need to help their people focus on the areas in which performance is so-so. This can require less effort while not taking your eyes off strengths development.

This is a perfect example of the old adage 'How do you eat an elephant?' You do so 'one bite at a time. Don't try to do so in one enormous bite.

5. Help employees align their strengths with the expectations and responsibilities of their roles.

In the best-case situations, team members' strengths should align with expectations, but sometimes things go a bit astray. Make sure you nurture and guide individuals to develop their core strengths and then give them goals aligned with their talent and responsibilities. You will have a better off team member as a result.

Importance of Aligning Organizational, Team, and Employee Goals

Organizational alignment is a key differentiator between high-performing and low-performing companies. In fact, research by LSA Global found that highly aligned companies grow revenue 58% faster and are 72% more profitable, and they outperform unaligned peers in employee engagement, customer satisfaction and retaining, and leadership.

Below are the key benefits of aligning goals in your organization:

1. Goals and values set the tone for your organizational strategy

Valures are ideals to which a person aspires. They may never be fully realized, but that doesn't mean we shouldn't strive to meet them. Values include things like 'honesty,' 'loyalty,' and 'creativity.

Organizational goals communicate what is important, and employees plan and execute their work based on those benchmarks. Organizational goals take the company's overall strategy and break it down into manageable chunks, providing checkpoints along the way to reach the general strategic mark.

2. Gives employees an idea of how their contributions work toward achieving team and organizational goals

It is easy for employees to feel lost and become disengaged once they don't understand where they fit in the organizational hierarchy. But when their goals are aligned with those of the corporate, they see the impact of their actions. It gives everyone a task to play and promotes accountability while providing natural points for recognition and celebration of excellent work.

3. Priorities are clarified

Employees have many tasks on their agenda every day, and they are trusted to settle on which should be accomplished first to move the organization forward. Once they understand how each task affects the team and organizational goals, it's easier for them to settle on the work that needs their attention first.

4. Aligned goals connect employees and teams

Alignment connects employees and teams to the organization and helps everyone get on the same page. Employees become disengaged once they feel they seem to be a one-person crew. But when everyone understands how their work is contributing to the organization's main goals, bonds form as everyone works together towards common goals.

How To Align Organizational Goals To Your Employees

Okay, so you now know that goal alignment is crucial, but how can you achieve it? Aligning your organization requires strong communication, leadership, and cooperation at every level. Here are some steps to achieve alignment on organizational, team, and employee goals.

1. Set clear organizational goals

Goals alignment starts at the top. Get together as a leadership team to debate the organization's vision and strategy, and identify the precise goals you would like to achieve as an organization. Get crystal clear on your objectives. Company goals should be targeted, strategic, and built around a vision the whole organization can share.

The clearer your goals are, the better others will know the vision and rally around a shared purpose. Vague or general goals cause vague or general results.

2. Get cooperation from higher leadership levels

Once you've got your organizational goals outlined, it's time to share them with leadership. Meet with senior and middle managers to talk about your vision and describe the precise goals and benchmarks you've identified for the organization.

Listen to their feedback and inquiries to make sure the goals add up and further refine your message. You'll need them to know and achieve these goals so as to effectively communicate them and drive alignment from the bottom up as well as the top down in your organization.

3. Communicate goals on every level

When goals and accountabilities are clear, employees are two times more likely to be highly engaged. Yet only 40% of employees across organizations know what their company's goals are. How are you able to get alignment and execute your objectives if half of your organization doesn't know what they're all working toward?

The key strategy is clear and consistent communication at every level of your organization.

Make goals a daily part of leadership meetings, team meetings, and employee one-on-ones, and performance reviews. Connect company initiatives and decisions to the underlying organizational goals. As you build goal conversations into your regular communications and messaging, you'll reinforce, remind, and align employees across the organization.

4. Help employees achieve their goals

Employees can't achieve in a vacuum. They need a team and organizational support to align and achieve their goals.

Support looks like this:

- Robust onboarding for a new employee to know their role, company goals, and where to go for support
- Ongoing employee training and development to build the talents and knowledge they have to succeed
- Resources and tools to effectively get the work done
- Regular feedback and training from managers to make sure work is on target and aligned
- Employees who have the support they have to succeed are better positioned to achieve goals that strategically align their work with company goals.

When employees understand what's expected of them, how their work fits into the bigger picture, and have the tools and resources they need to succeed, they're going to not only be aligned with the organization but engaged in their work.

CHAPTER THIRTEEN

DELIBERATE TRAINING AND TALENT MANAGEMENT

Talent Management is an organizational effort to attract, develop, and retain employees. Effective talent management solutions are seen in an organization's ability to attract and retain a variety of people with different abilities and skill sets that are paramount to the innovation, development, promotion, and sales of an organization's products or services to the market. When an organization is successful at managing its talent, the organization often meets the strategic goals and objectives essential to achieving a competitive advantage.

Components of Talent Management

Keeping employees engaged and motivated to stay with the organization long-term is the ultimate goal of talent management, that's achieved through a mixture of activities executed by both the HR function and management.

Talent acquisition, typically under the HR wheelhouse, is the gateway to talent management where initial employees are recruited and hired. Beyond the initial attainment of talent, there are five key activities made by an employee's manager that help keeps employee interest in working for an organization intact.

Onboarding

Initial employee training geared around fundamental organizational principles, job role requirements, and managing expectations is pivotal to early employee engagement and satisfaction. When employees have a transparent understanding of the organization, what their role encompasses, and what goals they're working toward to assist the corporate achieve success, they acclimate to their jobs faster and have a better sense of ownership over their performance.

Be intentional with employee onboarding. If the worker feels as if the work that he/she will contribute is valued by the organization as a whole, he/she is going to be more motivated to satisfy and exceed performance expectations, adapting to a replacement workplace climate with speed and excellence.

Employee Training Programs

All employees value the chance to refine and develop skills associated with their position. Training that's informative, engaging and simply accessible can help employees cultivate the knowledge required to assist them in becoming great at their jobs. When it involves training, the tactic of delivery, the standard of the training content, and therefore the frequency it's delivered are important aspects that management should prioritize when developing a talent management strategy.

Organize training regularly. Not only does ongoing training appease employee desire for improved efficiency and an understanding of existing responsibilities, but it satisfies a deeper desire for career advancement, which will be achieved through the event of critical skills in an employee's department. It also helps management raise awareness of the pace of change because the market grows and matures, ensuring that each employee is positioned to assist the organization in achieving success now and in the future as new technologies emerge.

Performance Evaluation And Management

Employees care the maximum amount as their managers do about their performance, and when they're in the dark, they're quick to feel unappreciated and undervalued, leading them to seek elsewhere for employment. Regular performance evaluations are essential to helping employees understand responsibilities, workload priorities, and the way their contributions impact the organization's success.

Give your employees public recognition when they've done a good job, don't wait until their annual review to give them kudos privately. In doing this, managers can highlight the tactics of high-performing employees, which will be emulated by others, also as to keep the worker or team that has been recognized satisfied and committed to continued excellence.

Succession Management

What does your top talent constantly have in mind? Advancement. High performers are motivated to achieve existing roles when the chance for advancement is within grasp. To retain talented employees, an organization must have opportunities for them to grow. To try to do this, management must keep a keen eye out for exemplary performers and make efforts to make sure they're set for fulfillment when a replacement position within the organization becomes available.

Be transparent with your top talent by letting them know that you simply see potential in them to assume a replacement role down the road. If employees see a future within the organization and are backed by a manager, they are committed to furthering their success; they're going to be much less likely to leave the organization for a replacement job.

Talent is the basis of any organization. To stay up with market demands, technological innovations, and, therefore, the changing industry landscape, an organization must maintain a variety of people who are gifted in several skill sets to sustain or obtain a competitive advantage. Thus, a sustained approach to managing talented employees is central to the survival of the business.

Benefits of Talent Management

Talent management is usually a discipline as much because the HR functions itself or a little bit of initiatives aimed toward people and organization development. Different organizations utilize talent management for their benefit. This is often as per the dimensions of the organization and their belief in the practice.

It could just include an easy interview of all employees conducted yearly, discussing their strengths and developmental needs. This might be utilized for checking the people against the longer-term initiatives of the organization and for succession planning. There are more benefits that are wide-ranged than those discussed above. The advantages are:

1. Right person in the right Job: Through a correct ascertainment of an individual's skills and strengths, people's decisions gain a strategic agenda. The skill or competency checking allows you to require a stock of skill inventories lying within the organization. This is often especially important both from the attitude of the organization, also that of the employee because the proper person is deployed in the right position, and employee productivity is increased. Also, since there's a far better alignment between an individual's interests and his job profile, work satisfaction is increased.

2. Retaining the best talent: Despite changes in the global economy, attrition remains a serious concern of organizations. Retaining top talent is vital to leadership and growth within the marketplace. Organizations that fail to retain their top talent are in the danger of losing bent to competitors. The main target is now on charting employee retention programs and methods to recruit, develop, retain and have interaction with quality employees. Employee growth in a career has got to be taken care of; while succession planning is being performed, those that are on the radar have to be kept in check in order that they know their performance is being rewarded.

3. Better hiring: The standard of an organization is the quality of the workforce it possesses. The simplest way to have talent at the highest level is to have talent at rock bottom. No wonder then, talent management programs and training, hiring assessments, became an integral aspect of HR processes nowadays.

4. Understanding employees better: Employee feedback gives deep insights to the management about their employees. Their development needs, career aspirations, strengths and weaknesses, abilities, likes and dislikes. It's easier, therefore, to work out what motivates them individually, and this helps many Job enrichment processes.

5. Better professional development decisions: When an organization gets to understand who its high potential is, it becomes easier to take a position in their professional development. Since development involves investment decisions towards learning, training and development of the individual either for growth, succession planning, performance management etc., an organization remains bothered about where to make this development and talent management just make this easier for them.

Apart from having robust talent management, experience also determines how organization rate their organizations as workplaces. In addition, if employees are positive about the talent management practices of the organization, they're more likely to have confidence in the way forward for their organization. The result is a more committed and engaged workforce determined to outperform their competitors and ensure a leadership position in the marketplace for their organization.

6. Smoother onboarding process: New recruits need a smooth transitional experience once they enter an organization. It is the HR's responsibility to make sure that the onboarding process is organized. If the onboarding process lacks clarity, then new employees are likely to be confused about their roles and their perception of the organization entirely. This is when talent management comes to their rescue. It enables HR to get down a focused onboarding strategy.

7. Retaining talent: In spite of all efforts taken by HR, it still gets difficult to retain employees, especially top performers, in the organization. They quit the organizations for greener pastures.

But, talent management enables HR to carry back employees through engagement and retention programs. HR also can take initiatives that foster employee growth.

8. Succession planning: It is a fact that you can't stop employees from leaving your organization. Their replacement must be found. Similarly, when employees are promoted or transferred, new vacancies are created. In both scenarios, talent management can help HR in succession planning and determine how vacant positions are often filled timely without affecting productivity and price.

9. Training and development: Talent management also helps HR to develop where you would like to introduce new training and development programs. HR can plan employee skill development courses, certifications and everyone or the other professional enhancement activities.

10. Improved Communication: Communication is the lifeline of any organization. If there are any communication issues, then it can damage the organization's function. One of the advantages of talent management includes promoting prompt and two-way communication between management and employees. When communication is effective, it also creates a positive impact on corporate improvement.

Connecting Talent Management Strategies

Talent management focuses on the premise that potential talents can be found using the performance management process and other sources like assessment centers. You can then run this identified talent through a group of developmental initiatives so that the people can be groomed to become leaders. What seems to be amiss? There's no way performance management factored into the talent process. Even those that are identified as leaders for key roles need to be assessed because that's the only way to know if they will be effective. The following is how these should be connected to ensure that your organization has effective leaders:

Regular Tracking Mechanism

Performance measurement doesn't stop with the talent being selected for a better role. You also need a daily tracking process that ensures that there's a feedback cycle factored in. This has to be embedded into the talent management process as well, to make sure that at every stage of leadership development, the people receiving feedback on their performance and the gaps to be addressed which will make sure that those who become leaders at the top of the method haven't only learned to leverage their strengths, but also be introspective on their weaknesses and the way to manage them.

Effective Parameters

When you assess performance, you have a group of parameters with which to gauge everyone on. These are usually a mixture of behavioral and functional elements. When the talent management process takes place, in other to make sure that the leaders are effective, the parameters need to be aligned to it. So ensuring that the parameters are well-linked to businesses that the leaders are expected to deliver on will be essential.

Two-way Communication

When someone is being developed as a leader, they need high aspirations and expectations from the talent management program and the HR team. Therefore, sometimes they could be keen to share the progress if they meet certain challenges. Ensuring that the communication process is usually two-way and open dialogue helps a lot. This ensures that your potential leaders won't consider exiting the firm due to any issues they face during the talent management process. Even as the performance management process works well when there are conversations, this process should also take the same approach. It can reduce or maybe prevent attrition.

Results Orientation

All aspects of the talent management approach should have a transparent results-based orientation. What this means is leaders who are a part of the event process should remember that results are what will make the difference. They're being groomed for bigger roles, and a few of the interventions could be essential for them to develop certain skills further. Even so, how they achieve the results that are expected from them or communicated to them is important.

People Management Skills Evaluation

To be an efficient leader, one of the most important qualities you need is a superb and approachable people manager. You have to trace that aspect in those that are a part of the talent management program. While many of them may have already exhibited these qualities when they were assessed during their performance appraisal, this needs a little bit of tracking during the developmental initiatives too. This is often because they're being put through learning interventions or projects, which may put them out of their temperature and that they are likely to react differently under stressful situations. So evaluating them on the talents that are associated with how they manage their teams and other people relationships in those circumstances is a great way to make them effective leaders.

Company Vision and Values Alignment

A person could be a superb performer and have the potential to grow further, but if they're misaligned to the values and vision of the organization, there'll be a significant problem at a later stage. It's important to assess this during the talent management phase so that if there are any red flags you should know, they will be uncovered early.

These are the performance-linked aspects that a possible leader who is a component of the succession planning program should be assessed on. Organizations should implement these checks into their talent management process so that they will make sure that the leaders, who are developed, are effective.

Why Training Is Important For Talent Management

Employees care whether an organization takes a real interest in their future. The emphasis here is on the word "genuine." Training should be something an organization devotes significant time, energy and resources to. This makes employees feel satisfied with their role in the organization.

They want the organization to take care of them, invest in their future, and ensure they grow and develop as people. In turn, employees are happier and more motivated to offer their best performance.

Training builds loyalty:

Training builds loyalty, and loyalty, in turn, builds productivity. When companies invest in their people, those people successively invest themselves in the company. And when an employee is loyal, he or she is more engaged, which leads to higher job satisfaction and more productivity.

Talented people want to advance:

Talented people value a company's support in the process. Motivated, ambitious employees want training, coaching, and mentoring. They need to become more valuable and versatile in the business world. There is no employee that doesn't appreciate the support that helps advance their career. If your company doesn't provide that support, rest assured, your top talent will soon find another employer that does.

Training corrects systemic weaknesses in your business:

Often, companies have one or two core areas of dysfunction that hold them back. Customer service, marketing and elements of the sales process are often areas where companies tend to fall significantly short. These weaknesses usually correspond to skill gaps, especially teams. Well-chosen training eliminates those weaknesses and takes the brakes off company growth.

Specialized coaching supercharges your top performers:

As much as we wish to believe business is a whole team effort, the truth is that few people in your organization who drive most of the growth and profits. If you identify these people and provide them the high-end coaching that helps them excel, you'll make an enormous difference to your organization.

Training fuels a culture of learning:

Nowadays, business moves fast. Markets shift, technologies change, and skill gaps widen. And changes are accelerating. The businesses that thrive are agile and adaptive; that's, companies that "learn" as organizations.

When you implement learning into your company culture (and you absolutely must), you have to place your money where your mouth is. Be generous with training budgets, cover the prices of self-learning materials and online courses, and fund employees' further training in situations where it can benefit your business. The initial cost upfront may be high, but the return on investment will be immensely more valuable.

What Makes Training Effective?

Organization training is a big topic, and lots of books have been written on training. However, a few core principles have stood the test of time. Give the right people the right training and at the right time. The more targeted and appropriate your training, the more your organization will benefit. The more disorganized it is, the more your time and money are wasted. Determine precisely where your skill gaps are and who exactly must be trained. Select programs that closely match your business's needs.

Training programs should be seen as the initiative to skill acquisition, not a one-time transformation. Employees must be ready to practice and use what they've learned to cement their skill set. Be certain they will apply their new skills, receive support and feedback, and be given enough time to build up their performance.

Most companies either neglect training or waste money on inappropriate programs without follow-up. Take the time to get your training right, and you stand to gain a true advantage in talent management.

Importance Of Employee Training

Employee training is a work program designed to equip employees with specific knowledge and skills to facilitate and improve job performance in current roles. However, while most organizations understand the importance of initial job training and training new employees, many neglect investing in continued training and development and pay a high price in lost talent, productivity and profits.

Quality employee training and development allows organizations to retain the right talent and boost profits. In this tight job market, competition for top talent is more competitive than ever. Recruiting quality employees takes time and money. How you train, develop talent directly impacts retention and growth. Effective employee training and development also contributes to a healthier organization overall.

Benefits of Employee Training and Development

1. Higher Productivity
Employee training implicitly empowers employees to be simpler and efficient at their jobs. It

also improves employee engagement which increases productivity.

2. Higher Employee Retention

A Harvard Business Review study found that the shortage of career development opportunities was a serious driver in job dissatisfaction and early exits. When employees feel that companies are investing in their futures instead of just their current job roles, they're more likely to reward the company with increased loyalty, engagement and productivity. Furthermore, people like feeling valued and being competent. When employees feel that they're important to an organization and are well prepared to do their jobs well, they need higher job satisfaction, resulting in lower rates of absenteeism and turnover.

3. Fewer Accidents

Training provides employees with the knowledge and skills they need to stop and handle any errors and accidents on the work.

4. Reduced Need For Constant Supervision (Less Micromanagement)

Well-trained employees are fully conscious of expectations, duties and responsibilities. Consequently, they require less expensive supervision, allowing your organization to devote these resources toward more strategic endeavors.

5. Securing Long-Term Organizational Success

Leadership has a huge impact on the success of any given organization. Consequently, preparing and retaining talent to fit into these roles is critical. Providing employees with better knowledge and skills prepares them to take your organization to the next level.

It's clear that quality employee training and development is crucial to organizational success. However, these programs don't just happen accidentally. They require careful planning and implementation.

6. Addressing Weaknesses

If an organization owner evaluates his workforce closely, he'll likely find out that some of his employees lack certain skills. A training program presents a chance to instill the needed skills in the employees. It also helps to expand the knowledge base of all employees.

7. Improved Performance Of Employees

An employee who receives training from time to time is in a better position to enhance his work productivity. Because of training programs, every employee will be well versed with the security practices and right procedures to follow when completing basic tasks. A training program also helps in building an employee's confidence since he will gain a far better understanding of the industry and the responsibilities of his role.

8. Boosts Company Profile and Reputation

As mentioned earlier, employee training isn't just good for the workers but also for the organization. Conducting frequent training and development programs is a method of developing the organization's employer brand, thus making it a major consideration for the highest employees working for competitor firms and graduates. An organization that trains its employees will be more attractive to potential new employees, particularly those looking to advance their skills.

9. Innovation

When employees receive consistent training, it fosters their creativity. The training programs help employees to be more independent and artistic when they encounter challenges in their work.

Steps To Making An Efficient Employee Training Program

1. Identify Your Business Goals

Evaluate your company's overall strategic goals. Then, use these goals to guide employment training design and development, which specialize in creating programs that have a measurable impact on goal attainment. A top-quality learning management system is the best way to ensure internal control, training and results.

2. Define Measurable Learning Goals and Objectives

Learning objectives should have long- and short-term measurable outcomes to gauge training effectiveness. Then, implement regular improvements to the methodologies as necessary. An efficient way to ensure employees are consistently meeting and exceeding objectives and expectations is to use a learning management system that has tracking, reporting, mapping, certification, and testing capabilities.

3. Find Skill Gaps

Determine how current employee behavior is impacting business goals. Also, analyze gaps between current and ideal skill sets to find out specific learning objectives. Ideally, your employee training plan should target three learning objective groups.

Re-Skill and/or Up-Skill: Providing opportunities for employees to re-skill or up-skill can prove vital for retention purposes and also for organizational survival. This is especially true as we continue to normalize operations and culture after the pandemic. These types of skilling can aid the organization to pivot and remain flexible to meet the challenges of the market.

Motivation: Identify why training is vital to employees beyond job function to motivate workers to shine at training initiatives. These learning objective groups should be applied to all or any areas of your organization training, including communication training for workers, employee engagement training, ethics training for workers, HR learning, and employee relations training, and critical training for brand spanking new managers and supervisors.

Critical Thinking: Providing critical knowledge and thinking methodologies to allow employees to excel in a manner that goes beyond department and job function for increased cross-functionality.

4. Layer Employee Training Methodologies

Use multilayered training activities to make long-term performance improvement by blending learning experiences and training methods to focus on essential business, customer and employee needs. The most effective training programs combine different learning elements to optimize the training experience.

You should also think about cross-training employees. Not only does this ensure cross-functionality between departments so that operations are never hooked into specific individuals. It also increases engagement, productivity and morale by making employees more invested in the operational bigger picture.

5. Post-Training Reinforcement

If your employee training program is merely used as a way to orientate your staff, you're doing yourself and your employees an enormous disservice. Not only will your employees forget everything they learned during the new employee orientation, but they'll also miss the chance to gain additional insight and truly grow. This is often where employee training comes into play. Ensure that your training goes above and beyond orientation by allowing employees to access it whenever and wherever they need it on their own devices.

Effective Employee Training Methods

To create a cheerful and productive workforce, training managers must provide opportunities for further training and growth. Unfortunately, too many employees or management dismiss training as boring or unnecessary. And, let's face it, employee training is often boring, but only if the wrong type of training is matched up with the subject or issue, you're tackling. Matching the kinds of employee training to your employee needs can ensure they receive the knowledge they need in the format best fitted to it.

The most effective employee training methods for your employees are:

1. Instructor-led training

Instructor-led training is a traditional type of employee training that takes place in a classroom, with a trainer or instructor doing the training. This is a highly effective method of employee training, especially for complex topics. Instructors can answer specific employee questions or direct them to more resources.

However, instructor-led training has some disadvantages, such as cost and time to implement. It also can be unnecessary for concise topics.

2. eLearning

eLearning is primarily based online relies on online videos, tests, and courses to deliver employee training. Employees can do their training right in the palm of their hand with a smartphone or on their company computers.

It's one of the simplest types of employee training to roll bent larger populations, especially for workers who are remote or have high turnover rates. With interactive games, tests, videos, activities, or maybe gamified components, it also can go an extended way towards keeping your employees engaged with the training.

Of course, eLearning also has its own challenges. Without a solid instructional design strategy behind it, the graphics and visuals that make eLearning fun also can make it gimmicky or quickly outdated. Keeping it up-to-date is additionally a necessary best practice. We cover the main advantages, and drawbacks, of eLearning here.

3. Simulation employee training

Simulation training is most frequently provided through a computer, augmented, or computer game device. Despite the initial costs for producing that software or technology, however, simulation training is often a necessary option for workers in riskier or high-stakes fields. You'll often see simulation training for pilots or doctors, but it is often useful for other employees too.

This type of employee training is highly effective and reliable, allowing employees to progress consistently and at their own pace.

4. Hands-on training

Hands-on training includes any experiential training that's focused on the individual needs of the worker. It's conducted directly on the work. Hands-on training can help employees fit perfectly into their upcoming or current role while enhancing their current skills.

One advantage of hands-on training is that it is applied immediately to the employees' jobs. They're also effective for training when it involves new business equipment and procedures."

This is a time-intensive method of employee training; however, that's best used when there are enough resources available to support employees during the program. Learn more about experiential learning here.

5. Lecture-style training

Important for getting big chunks of data to an outsized employee population, lecture-style training is often a useful resource for communicating required information quickly.

However, you should use this type of employee training sparingly as it is believed to be the least amount effective of all training methods. In many cases, lectures contain no type of interaction from the trainer to the trainee and may be quite boring. Studies show that people only retain 20 percent of what they're taught in a lecture.

6. Group discussions and activities

For the right group of employees, group discussions and activities can provide the right training option. It allows multiple employees to be coached directly in an environment that better fits their current departments or groups. These discussions and activities are often instructor-led or facilitated by online prompts that are later reviewed by a supervisor.

This type of employee training is best used for challenges that need a collaborative approach to complex issues.

7. Role-playing

Similar to group discussions, role-playing specifically asks employees to figure through one aspect of their jobs during a controlled scenario. They'll be asked to think about different points of view and think on their feet as they run through the role-playing activity.

Like other group activities, role-playing is very effective but could also be unnecessary for easy, straightforward topics. It also requires more employee time, potentially taking time away from a whole department while they're undergoing the training.

8. Management-specific activities

Management-specific activities are employee training focused on the requirements of managers. They include simulations, brainstorming activities, team-building exercises, role-playing, or focused eLearning on management best practices.

While management training can include many various types of training, it is important to think about the extra needs of your managers separately from the remainder of your employee population. This ensures they have the inspiration they have to support the remainder of their staff.

9. Case studies or other required reading

Some employee training topics are readily accessible through required readings. Case studies, especially, can provide a fast way for workers to find out about real workplace issues. Employees can read through these at their own pace or while working in a team-building session with other employees.

Case studies are a great option for focused topics, but more complex topics will likely require more advanced types of employee training.

Types Of Training

The various types of training given to the workers of the organization are as follows:

Induction Training: This is training that is given to a new employee at the time when they join an organization. This training is given to them to build up their confidence in the organization and offer them information about the varied procedures, rules and regulations. They're introduced to their work environment and other employees in other to create a feeling of belongingness and loyalty amongst them.

Job Training: This is given in several ways to make the workers proficient in handling various machines, equipment and materials so that their operations are smooth and faultless and accidents on the work are often avoided.

Crafts Training: Craftsmanship training involves teaching a selected craft thoroughly and making an employee become a competent craftsman. The extent and intensity of coaching vary from craft to craft. Apprenticeship training is a major method adapted for such type of training.

Promotional Training: The existing talented employees could also be given adequate training to make them eligible for promotion to higher jobs within the organization. The aim of such training is to make the workers fit to undertake higher job responsibili-ties.

Refresher Training: This is meant for the old employees of the organization. Its purpose is to acquaint the existing workforce with the newest methods of performing their jobs and improve their efficiency further.

PART THREE

LEADERSHIP IN CHALLENGING TIMES

CHAPTER FOURTEEN

LEADERSHIP CHALLENGES

Leaders are likely to face series of leadership challenges every day, from all sides, around every corner, even from within. Leadership based on authenticity and meaningful relationships takes courage. This is the type of leadership that inspires others, serves others, and points them toward a greater purpose and vision.

There are many bumps on the road of leadership. Sometimes they're mere roadblocks, and sometimes they're bridges. But every challenge is a chance, an opportunity to find out about yourself, improve your skills and strengthen your emotional intelligence, which is so critical to effective leadership.

There are many types of leadership challenges, and we'll be discussing them below:

Self Challenges

The first and most persistent source of leadership challenges is you. Yes, there are many external forces that will throw obstacles in your path. But most frequently, it's our own thoughts, feelings and ways of reacting to situations that will create the biggest hurdles in leadership. What are the ways to overcome self challenges?

Stay Humble: When you're in a position of leadership, it is often easy to start out believing your own press. Maybe things are going great. You're hearing accolades. It's easy to start out believing that each one of these success is your doing. that perhaps, just maybe, it's you who deserves the credit for your organization's greatest accomplishments.

But I don't need to tell you that an arrogant leader isn't someone anyone would like to follow. That's a leader who alienates their team, causes conflict and incites drama. None of which is healthy for an organization.

The best leaders are humble leaders. They know that leadership is about influence and impact, not authority. They recognize the worth of the team around them. And that they reap the rewards of a team that respects their character and willingly works alongside them to succeed in a standard goal.

It is often a challenge to remain humble as a leader, but it's an important leadership quality that's worth fighting for.

Have Self-Confidence: Most leaders could struggle with self-doubt in the face of self-challenges. And the more a leader succeeds, the more they're likely to wrestle with the feeling that they're not really who people think they are. This is referred to as imposter syndrome, and it is often a very painful challenge for several leaders because it creates a lot of self-doubts. It can cripple your ability to inspire, motivate and serve your team.

That's why healthy self-confidence is an important characteristic of leadership. Whereas humility is about knowing you're not the center of the world, self-confidence means understanding that you bring value to the world. It's about quieting the inner voice that tells negative things like you you're failing, you're not okay, or you're a fraud. When self-doubt says you're not enough, self-confidence says, "I am enough."

Follow Through: Leaders are busy. There are lots of things to do and never enough time to do it. Distractions, emergencies and new opportunities pull you in various directions. This is why it isn't surprising that one leadership challenge you would possibly face is a tough time following through on the plans, ideas and methods you set in place. In fact, some studies suggest that 90% of strategic plans fail to meet expectations.

Yes, there's plenty of things to be done. There are changes and surprises. But taking over such a lot that you're unable to end what you started has hamstrung the effectiveness of the many leaders before you.

Deal With Stress And Anxiety: With all of the leadership challenges staring you in the face, you'd be within your rights to feel stressed. It's natural. But the anxiety these leadership challenges create can itself be a big challenge to your leadership. The fear, the self-doubt, the cascade of problems and expectations that leaders often face can all add up to A level of stress that puts your ability to lead in peril.

Because we act differently in times of stress, it's tough to remain focused. We could become angry and fall back on the defense—it's the fight-or-flight response that will effectively short down our rational brain.

That is why it is usually valuable for leaders to find out more about how they react to worry, understand their behaviors, and better avoid the pitfalls to leadership that happens when anxiety goes unchecked.

Stay Motivated: Everyone has bad days, the days when progress is slow, or an attempt fails, and you fall under a funk. It's easy to linger over what isn't working and let it sap your energy, which is often especially tough for a leader to figure out because everyone's looking to you to be a cheerleader.

Sometimes just the expectation of you to be the chief motivator is often one of the most demotivating factors that affect you. But your team is looking to you to steer, guide and encourage them.

Avoid Burnout: When you lose motivation, you could begin to burn out entirely. We've already talked about some leadership challenges, and with all of this against you, how can you not burn yourself out as a leader?

This is a big challenge. And to be perfectly frank, burnout gets the most of plenty of leaders. They push too hard, never rest, and spend insane hours working. But if you burn yourself out, you're not leading anyone. I witness plenty of this working with high-performing leaders. It's tempting to want to play a superhero, but if you're not taking care of yourself, how will you be able to lead and encourage others?

This is why self-care is vital. It helps prevent burnout and refocus you on what's important. The same thing can be said for your teams.

Vulnerability: Let's bring this full back circle because vulnerability is closely tied to humility. And it's equally important to good leadership.

It takes plenty of intestinal fortitude to say admit that you were wrong. It takes high emotional intelligence to admit your mistakes, ask for feedback and learn from criticism. If you're unable to ask for help, it is often a serious hurdle to effective leadership.

Perhaps being vulnerable even encompasses all of the interior challenges we've talked about. Because vulnerability is about authenticity, it means having an accurate picture of yourself. Knowing what brings you down and what keeps you going. Being real about what you're feeling. Engaging in good conversations with your team and being willing to point out your weakness.

It is hard to do, which is why many leaders like to project invulnerability. But that's a trap. Great leaders take the challenge to be vulnerable, own it and live it.

Ability Testing Challenges

It is not only internal challenges you face as a leader. Some leadership challenges come right down to the variability of skills it takes to lead effectively. The strengths you have to create and the approaches you have to find out if you're going to make the type of impact great leaders make on their teams.

Most skills can be learned, honed and improved. Some take more work than others. But every challenge to your skills and skills as a leader is a chance to take yourself and your team to the next level. How do you tackle the challenges that test your leadership abilities?

Keep Your Team Motivated And Inspired: I have discussed with you the challenges of keeping yourself motivated. It is often challenging to keep your team motivated. Every day, the people you lead will as, "Why?" What's the vision? Where are we going?

As a leader, it is your responsibility to keep your team focused on the purpose. To inspire them with a shared vision and encourage them as you accomplish your goals together.

But it isn't always easy. When you're not feeling very inspired yourself, or you're unsure how things are going to end up. Your team could be struggling, and you'll be struggling with how to rekindle their spirit. People are people; we're emotional beings with highs and lows. And it's up to the leader to inspire and motivate their team through all of these times.

Reward and Recognize Employees: Another crucial aspect leaders can't overlook is a solid reward and recognition program for their teams. Sometimes, this means following your company's established program, but it doesn't mean you have to stop there.

The key to any worthwhile program is recognizing employees the way they desire. This can be a pat on the back, time off, a nice little piece of hardware to sit on their desk, or maybe a little bonus at the end of the year.

Manage People And Resources: Manage, not micromanage. That distinction itself is another leadership challenge.

Navigating the complexities of interpersonal relationships and handling team dynamics brings daily pressures of excellent decision-making as a reward for your organization's resources. All of that bound up into a bundle of challenges will tie you into knots if you let it.

And don't ditch delegation. Delegating is straightforward. Delegating well isn't. When you do the right thing, delegating isn't about simply "handing things off" or "clearing your plate." It's about empowering others to do the work you've brought them on board to do.

Taken together, all the stress of managing resources well can present a deep challenge for you as a leader.

Build Your Own Skills: The more you spend time and energy helping your team grow and develop their skills, the harder it is to intentionally develop your own. At the danger of sounding as anti-servant-leadership, you can't only look out for others and not look out for your own growth and development.

Actually, it's related in a way to the challenge of avoiding burnout. Even as you have to make sure you're getting enough emotional rest and self-care, you have to make sure you can secure your own intellectual and professional well-being.

Make Changes: Change is a constant phenomenon. This has recently become a cliché, but a long time ago, it was a profound philosophy. And it's true. If there's one thing we can calculate, especially in this day and age, things will always change.

Sometimes change is predictable. More often, it's not. The challenge for the leader is to supply consistency and clarity through it all.

Make Tough Decisions: There's always an easy way of out all challenges, but most of the time, it is never the right choice. Leadership is filled with tough decisions, some gut-wrenching. It's the leader's job to handle those tough decisions.

That can be hard. But even harder is the thought of living with the choices you've made. There'll be consequences. Physics tells us that for each action, there's an equal and opposite reaction. And hard decisions aren't too different. The choice you make might end up being a nasty call. But you need to make the decision—often with little or no time to think through all the eventualities.

You can easily change some decisions if you have to. But there's a good chance the toughest decisions accompany no take-backs. You make your bed and dwell on it. Great leaders can make those difficult decisions and sleep through the night afterward.

Communication Challenges

There are internal leadership challenges; there are also challenges that stretch your skills and abilities. But we can argue that communication challenges are the biggest of them all. Plenty of information can be skipped, jumbled or misinterpreted. And when there's faulty communication, people will fill the gaps with their own assumptions.

Communication presents many leadership challenges. Below are effective ways to tackle them:

Keep Everyone Informed: Your employees are individuals who come from different backgrounds and bring different experiences and feelings to the table; it's a challenge to get all of them facing the same direction.

How do you confirm there's common understanding of what you are doing and why you are doing it? How do you get everyone facing the same direction instead of following their own agendas? It's critical for the success of your organization to have alignment with a standard vision, purpose, and understanding of what it means to win. And it takes continuous attention and communication to make it happen.

Tackle Conflicts Early: Conflicts are the drama that spills over when under-the-table agendas that drive numerous unhealthy behaviors in our organizations meet one another in battle. The same can be said when differences of opinion get personal.

Conflict is a component of life. And it's most definitely a part of any organization. It's also a chance for the visceral brain to pull the cord on our fight-or-flight response with the result that we either avoid conflict (which results in problems) or dig in our heels for a good, old-fashioned brawl (which results in problems).

Effective leadership means embracing the very fact that conflict has to happen. However, this also means there's a need for constructive conflict, not destructive conflict. It means tough conversations sometimes it hurts, but conflict is often incredibly healthy for an organization that's willing to grow out of it. It's up to you because the leader has to lead conflicts toward productive resolution.

And remember, problems don't get better with time. Resolving issues early means that you could stop a small spark before it causes a forest fire.

Be Bold To Give Bad News: Life isn't all sunshine and rainbows. We all know this. But that doesn't make it any easier to be the bearer of bad news. Things don't always go as planned. Mistakes happen, and problems need to be addressed. Sometimes leadership means having to deliver the bad news about what went wrong or what must change.

It is the leader's calling to be clear and decisive. Empathy is vital, but so is clarity and understanding. The bad news is often dramatic—it's your job to deliver it and manage it in a way that stifles drama before it contaminates your culture.

Challenges Of Crisis

Speaking of bad news, sometimes the most important challenges come when the unexpected happens. A natural disaster, an economic upheaval, a failed product launch, a catastrophic mistake, losing an employee, or even a worldwide pandemic like the coronavirus.

Those are the days when we most need to intensify as leaders. And they're the pressure-cooker moments that expose just how hard effective leadership is. Crisis leadership can challenge you like nothing else. But it also can bring out the best in great leaders. Let's look at some of the leadership challenges that rear their heads during tough times:

Being Positive: It's far too tempting to be negative. During a time of crisis, it's not impossible that you feel negative. However, your team must see hope. Not false hope or unrealistic optimism, but it doesn't hurt to see the opportunities in challenges or the light in dark times.

Exhibiting leadership in tough times takes a great measure of patience and empathy. It means working more diligently to rally the team, learn from adversity, and celebrate your wins. It takes diligence not to blame or point fingers. It is a time to be keen on sharing your purpose and vision even more.

Teams look to their leaders as a beacon in difficult circumstances. This could be hard for you because you have to model the positivity they're looking for.

Being Clear And Good: It is tempting to sugarcoat things or withhold information. Perhaps there is a real danger to the organization, and you should rather insulate your team from it. But the best way to lead through a crisis is to prioritize clarity over comfort. Be real and transparent. It's not the easiest thing to do by any means.

Be Calm: Remember the fight-or-flight response? That's where your amygdala (part of the visceral brain where emotions are processed) goes on alert in the face of danger, whether it's physical or psychological.

Times of crisis are usually a trigger for your amygdale. So it is a big challenge to remain calm, let alone model and encourage calmness for all those in your care when it seems like the odds are against you. But that's exactly what your people need to see from you when the going gets tough. They have to be sure you are a leader who stays levelheaded during a crisis.

Be Human: You're not a machine; you're human. Your employees understand that and that they need to see it.

It is often easier to show off the human part of you and just tackle the challenges you're facing as rationally and methodically as possible. There's nothing wrong with that. But you're human, and the people you lead are humans too. As difficult as it is to admit, being human and allowing yourself to be vulnerable can be one of the best examples you set for your team.

CHAPTER FIFTEEN

OVERCOMING GENERAL LEADERSHIP CHALLENGES

Developing Your Decision-Making Framework

The better you're at making decisions, the higher you'll overcome the leadership challenges you'll face. And how do you get better at making decisions?

You have to start by understanding your attitudes and beliefs, distilling them into a transparent purpose for yourself and your organization, and making that the measure for your decision-making. The following are tips to help you:

Get clear on your purpose: Define why you exist as an organization and what it means to be at your best as a leader.

Clarify your vision: Confirm you and your team understand what winning looks like.

Define your values: What are the nonnegotiable, deeply held values which will cause doing all of your best work within the way you think in doing it?

Use your purpose, vision and values to guide your decision-making. When you're facing leadership challenges, it is often easy to become reactive, to only put out fires as you see them. But if you give yourself a transparent framework for making decisions in good times and in tough times, you'll be ready to handle challenges from an edge of clarity and selection. You'll stay aligned with the larger purpose you're aiming for. And you'll also be able to proactively handle leadership challenges because you've already determined how to approach them.

Operate Without Fear

Fear isn't unhealthy until you let it run the show. That's when our old flame, the amygdala, takes an excessive amount of control and rational thought goes out the window. Fear-based leadership isn't leadership at all; it's where bad decisions happen.

And fear isn't always the same as being afraid. Many people will likely say they're not fearful. We're courageous leaders, willing to do anything. But here's the truth, regardless of who we are, what proportion of authority we have, and what position we're in, at heart, we are a scared little kid. We're stressed, unsure of ourselves, trying to find approval, and fearing failure.

To understand who you are, acknowledge the fears and insecurities you face. Develop an idea and base it on your decision-making frame. When you do this, fear won't have any choice but to get behind you.

Prioritize Your Efforts

Sometimes, there is plenty of things to do. That's where you have to take stock and set some priorities.

There's an idea called the Pareto principle, or the 80/20 rule. It's a principle that says 80% of the consequences come from only 20% of the causes. It translates into leadership, too. As a leader, 80% of your impact comes from 20% of what you are doing.

That means you have to seek out that 20% that makes the bulk of the impact and put those efforts at the very top of your list. Think of everything that you must do. Now (mentally or on paper), rank all of them on a scale from 1-10, where one is the highest priority, and ten is the lowest.

Look at that list. There's a lot there, but the Pareto principle tells us that only what's in spots one and two will really make the most impact. You are numbers three to seven are worthwhile, but eight to ten don't probably don't deserve much time at all. The first and second are where the most important difference is often made.

The problem is, when we don't assess our efforts, we frequently find ourselves spending plenty of time on the tasks, projects or decisions that won't have the impact to unravel our leadership challenges. But once you prioritize your efforts to get numbers one and two done, that's where the impact will be made.

Create A Psychologically Safe Environment

Your best work happens when people feel safe enough to have the conversations that matter with you.

But that type of psychological safety is a rare thing to find in many organizations. It takes plenty of effort to make it happen. It takes commitment and a willingness on everyone's part to interact in real conversations. Building an environment of safety requires transparency. People will only feel that type of safety in an environment of high trust. How can you build a psychologically safe environment?

A good place to start is to be great at listening. You have to make sure your people are heard. They have to understand they have a voice; they have to understand the matter.

When your team knows that you're listening, once they know their voice matters, great things can happen. They'll be more engaged. They'll care more, serve better and work harder. Not out of fear or compulsion, but because they know they're a part of something the entire team is working toward. Because they know you care about them and value them, you'll all be heading in the same direction—which means leadership won't be about trying to push people harder to satisfy goals but pulling them along by offering a vision and mission they will follow.

When you're all working toward the same goal, everyone knows their voice matters, and they see the support of leaders who believe in raising those around them; that's where you build trust. And trust creates a psychologically safe environment where your best people are happy to talk, wanting to push forward and excited to take on any challenge.

Develop A Growth Mindset

Great leaders know that leadership isn't about arriving at a destination. Leadership is about influence and impact, which means it's a journey that doesn't end. The best leaders, those who are well prepared to overcome the leadership challenges that come their way, are the leaders who can adapt. They're the leaders who never stop learning and always search for ways to enhance themselves.

Great leaders are humble, hungry and smart. Great leaders have a mindset of continual growth. And when a growth-minded leader faces challenges, they will adapt, learn from them and emerge even better equipped to tackle the next one.

PART FOUR

LEADERSHIP AND SELF CARE

CHAPTER SIXTEEN

LEADERSHIP: THE IMPORTANCE OF SELF-CARE

As a leader, it is important that you look out for yourself positively and effectively, not only for your employees but your loved ones too.

Successful leaders make self-care a priority so that they can perform at their best. What habits and routines have you ever established for yourself that have enabled your success? You have risen to where you're now because you're driven and determined to have a positive impact, but what are you doing for yourself so that you'll always be at your best?

As a productive, driven leader, you might not have enough time to devote to self-care. You prioritize work and family, which can feel selfless and honorable but can't create enough time to take better care of yourself.

Believe me, and I understand the feelings of devoting most of your time to your leadership role—at work. The reality is that such devotion is unsustainable. Leaders who fail to create time for self-care burn out quickly. They aren't fitted to long-term success, and they are characterized by a continuing feeling of being overwhelmed. Leaders who operate in this way don't lead effectively, nor do they serve as a good example for their people and the future leaders they ought to be focused on developing.

I think we can all agree that some amount of self-care is important for everybody, especially leaders who want to work in a consistent manner and guide their organizations to greatness. However, every individual is different, so what might work for might not work for someone else in the same or different department or another organization. With that in mind, there are some basic aspects of self-care which is adaptable to any leader or any leadership situation.

For starters, your self-care routine should involve a balanced approach that takes both your body and mind under consideration. I also recommend that it includes aspects of your social and spiritual lives that you can apply to specific situations. But first, I would like to discuss with you the biggest thing that stands between you and a healthy self-care routine: Time.

The Time Factor

The idea of self-care for leaders is a difficult paradox: Leaders have the least amount of time available to devote to self-care, and yet they're the people that often need self-care the most.

I would be surprised if this paradox didn't resonate with you. Most leaders I engage with are eager and excited to enhance themselves and their skills, but they keep running into barriers imposed by a lack of personal time in their schedule.

The truth is that you may never get the extra time you need for self-care. So, it's important to make the most of the time you have. Protect this time; don't let it get pushed down your calendar, only to get pushed into next week (or next month or even next year!). Time dedicated to self-care is as important as time dedicated to critical meetings or team initiatives within the workplace, so please treat it intrinsically.

Once you begin practicing self-care on a more consistent basis, you'll begin to integrate it into everything you are doing. In fact, I might argue that this Is the whole essence. It is not just about carving out time for self-care but about integrating self-care into everything you are doing.

Before you reach that time in your self-care journey, you have to improve your ability to remain fresh, rested and feeling good by following the following self-care strategies:

Develop A Consistent Sleep Pattern

When was the last time you had a very great night of sleep? It's been a long time. For several leaders, a restful night of sleep is extremely difficult to get. For some, it seems impossible. That's because most leaders and other people generally fail to prioritize sleep.

Get rid of staying up to burn the midnight oil, and don't force yourself to wake before dawn so you'll be the first one online or at the office. Create a nightly bedtime routine and make sure to schedule some wind-down time in the hours approaching that bedtime. Make it a habit to go to bed at approximately the same time every night.

Ensure your sleep time doesn't include searching social media or finishing last-minute work tasks which will fire you up or help calm you down before a restful night of sleep. Whenever you feel tempted to sabotage your sleep, you must stick with your healthy routine. This is one of the main keys to overall well-being that a lot of leaders ignore, and my advice to you is to implement a positive change. Your success and health depend on it.

Focus On Regular Exercising

Like sleep, exercise is another pillar of self-care for leaders. Again, I feel it's critically important to build your routines around exercise that fit best for you. Turning it into a habit makes it more likely that you will persist with it, and you are more likely to get the maximum advantages from it.

To give yourself the best chance of success, start small and take deliberate steps to realize your ultimate fitness goals. It's not about having the right body, having the ability to lift heavy weights or run a mile at a particular pace. Instead, it's about making your physical health a priority, regardless of the physical activity of choice.

An additional benefit is that once you build exercise into your self-care routine, you make it easier to get a good night's sleep on a more consistent basis. Plus, it'll boost your overall energy levels.

Eat Healthily

Sometimes people pay more attention to what they put into their cars than what they put in their bodies. Leaders are not any exception!

I like to consider food as fuel for the machine, referred to as the physical body. When you give the machine unhealthy fuel, you suffer, and your body sputters. But when you fill your tank with healthy whole foods and drinks with minimal processing, you give the machine of your body a foothold. It's like trading in an old beater for a brand-new sports car.

Lastly, a healthy body results in a healthy mind and clarity of thought. You'll have more energy and knowledge and less fatigue and tiredness.

Practice Gratitude

Psychologically speaking, there are few things more powerful than gratitude when it involves practicing self-care.

Our brains are naturally wired to see the negative first, which is why some leaders are often focused on what's wrong as against what's right or going well. This creates a negative, self-perpetuating psychological state that increases stress and strain while sapping energy and decreasing a leader's ability to think rationally.

Practicing gratitude can stop this negative process in its tracks. When you take time to be grateful for things you have achieved, you train your brain to make your world more positive, realistic, and healthy. When your brain swims in a sea of negativity, it can cause you to lead ineffectively. But when you are grateful, you'll operate with plenty of inspiration and positive energy.

Establish Healthy Boundaries

Here is a little secret I wish more leaders were aware of: You do not need to say "yes" to everything because you're the leader and are in a position of influence. You're in the position to decide timelines and deliverables, so discuss your responsibilities openly and do no agree to things that may hinder you or your team from fulfillment.

One of the quickest ways to deteriorate your physical, emotional, and mental health is to bite more than you can chew. It's okay to say "no" to things that don't align with your strategic priorities. Your leadership is going to be more consistent, energized and galvanizing when you practice discernment. It's hard not to say "yes" to everything, but I urge you to take charge and find healthy boundaries for yourself and others.

Have Quality Personal Time

I have been with countless leaders who felt like they needed permission to have fun or enjoy themselves. I have also been with leaders who have no iota of idea what they enjoy or how they want to spend their free time.

Don't be the leader who devotes yourself so fully to work that you eventually lose yourself in it. You're a person with a life outside the workplace, so ensure you live your life to its fullest.

I encourage you to focus on what you actually enjoy in life. How do you wish to spend your time? Are you spending any time doing the things you love? Or are you sacrificing fun and delight so as to devote more time to work?

Determine what gives you joy, pleasure, richness, and fulfillment in life. Then spend some time doing those things. Yes, you're busy, but that doesn't mean your free time should be spent worrying about how busy you're. It should be spent living life in a way that energizes and refreshes your life.

The Leadership Magnifying Effect

As leaders, we offer direction and leadership to our team members on a daily basis. This working relationship often involves significant communication and interaction. This means that our leadership behavior has a direct impact on the people we lead a day. Our self-care doesn't just impact us but impacts others around us as well. If we're having a nasty day, it's not just us that suffer, the people around us do too.

But that's not where it ends. As leaders, we give presentations, lead meetings and handle other teams and stakeholders. When we're not at our best, we're impacting the people outside of our teams too.

This all has the potential to magnify the impact of our leadership behavior. When we get angry or stressed, many of us feel it. If we're at our best, our people feel that too. This can send effects through the workplace. It really depends on just what type of effects we are making. Are they positive or negative?

Effects Of Lack Of Self Care

A lack of self-care at work can have various impacts. When we don't care for ourselves, we are more likely to feel stressed, unhappy, tired, overwhelmed, and cranky; all of those feelings can cause havoc for ourselves and for our teams. When it becomes a consistent pattern to neglect our self-care, we are more likely to face one or more of the following problems."

1. Inconsistent Leadership Behavior

Getting angry at work is one of the signs of a stressed, the overwhelmed leader is and shows inconsistent leadership behavior. Inconsistent behavior comes in many forms and poses a big threat to team culture.

At some point, you call out bad behavior, and the next day you overlook it. Perhaps you emphasize you're specialization in top-quality work one week, and then you ditch it subsequent.

You might even get angry at your team when you normally wouldn't. When you show inconsistent leadership behavior, your team won't know what to expect. This creates the potential for poor team culture because bad behavior goes unpunished. Team members start to feel scared of how you would react, so that they become tentative, walking on eggshells around you.

All this results in a nervous team that feels uncertain about what to expect. Pro-activity will suffer as team members wait to ascertain how you respond on a given day instead of stepping forward and taking the initiative.

2. Lack Of Empathy

When you feel overwhelmed, tired, stressed, or unhappy, how focused are you on the needs of others? Probably not much. Whenever I feel stressed or overwhelmed, my immediate focus will be on myself instead of the people around me. This is often damaging because your team needs your support.

When you are distracted by your own concerns, you're less likely to be interested in the welfare of others. Empathy suffers because you're more bound up in your own problems than those of your team members.

This can cause a situation where your team members feel they don't have your support; hence, they are less likely to return to you for support next time because it looks like you don't care.

3. Loss Of Confidence

Everyone wants to have a boss who was really capable, fun and a pleasure to be with. Unfortunately, the pressures of the workplace and personal toxic behaviors could cause leaders to lose confidence.

This loss of confidence can cause leaders to doubt themselves and get things wrong all the time. You could end up working longer and longer hours, trying desperately to fix the issues.

All you need to do is face up for yourself and focus your abilities, not continue to feel worse about yourself and watch your leadership suffer. This can eventually result in employee turnover if the teams don't see things getting any better.

Team members can see when their leader is struggling. When this persists for too long, team members start to wonder why they still put up with it and why they won't rebel. Ensuring you are the best leader you can give your team confidence in your leadership.

CONCLUSIONS

The topic and concept of leadership are among the most discussed topics in the world today, and rightly so. As a result of this, many opinions, concepts, and strategies have been generated about the subject, which sometimes makes it difficult for people who want to practice active leadership to learn and thrive. Many have argued that leaders are born and not made; others are of the opinion that some people are born leaders, while others believe that some leaders have leadership thrust upon them as a result of circumstances.

Often, leadership has been idealized, discussed, and described as a difficult thing making it difficult and seemingly unattainable for anyone aspiring to become a better leader. Regardless of the category or opinions generated about Leadership, it is certain that all leaders share a certain attribute that makes them leaders worthy of being followed. In fact, you will find that most people already possess these attributes and are likely to develop them and teach others till you become a complete leader. This book, therefore, seeks to help leaders who intend to improve in terms of these attributes to scale and advance their careers and lives.

Have you ever felt the urge to be better, improve and advance in life and your career, especially as a leader? Well, you are not alone, as even the greatest of leaders have always felt this way. In fact, I make bold to say that you read this book with the intention of improving and getting better to begin with. This desire or urge is usually what precedes change and improvement, which is necessary for cultivating the necessary skills needed to advance in your life and career. Most times, leaders are overwhelmed by the challenges they are faced with and often question their capabilities. This has led to leaders having to cope with the demands of their role and navigating through the doubts or desires, which has spurred them to seek advancement and development in leadership in the first place.

Becoming an effective and all-around leader is never easy, and as such, it takes time, effort and consistency. People who argue that leaders are made from experience might be right. However, leadership takes more than staying at the helm of affairs for a couple of years. Leadership is the deliberate desire to change and be better. Leadership is borne out of the desire to help others grow in terms of their career and achieve a common goal.

Companies, firms, and establishments are searching for leaders with the ability to be dynamic, spontaneous, resourceful, resilient, and emotionally intelligent. Indeed, it is rare for an individual to have the perfect blend of all these, but with the principles embedded in this book and the desire to effect change which is borne out of proactiveness, you will become the perfect leader, which you know you are capable of becoming.

Leaders are often faced with the challenge of channeling their desire for change, growth, and more innovativeness in the right direction. This is because, most times, there is a high tendency to misplace these desires, misconstrue them and channel them inappropriately. Therefore, this book seeks to help leaders embrace the change needed to grow and develop into the leader they know they are capable of becoming. Therefore, this book focuses on how to develop better leadership qualities across all spheres of life by helping its readers communicate more effectively, grow their level of confidence, and help them become more functional as a leader. Since this book is targeted at leaders, it concentrates on developing the attributes and characteristics necessary to forge the complete leader who can affect the change needed in an organization.

This book was written not only for leaders but also for anyone aspiring to be and advance or develop in his career. This book offers steps and strategies needed for individuals to gain the competence required to advance their lives and careers. This book focuses on communication, self-care, self-development, and employee management, which will make you a dynamic leader in the process. Should you decide to use the tips, strategies, and ideas reeled out through this book, you would have acquired the competence and skillsets needed to impose yourself as a leader and advance in life and your career. The book carefully unpacks salient yet vital information that is not obtainable in formal schools but is acquired through years of experience in the simplest way possible, thus providing great value for leaders and anyone who reads it.

REFERENCES

10 ways of building trust as a leader. Leaders.com. (2021, July 23). https://leaders.com/articles/company-culture/building-trust/.

21 effective ways to keep employees happy and productive - localwise. Localwise Jobs. (2019, March 21). https://www.localwise.com/a/1008-21-effective-ways-to-keep-employees-happy-and-productive.

360-Degree feedback: What is it and how does it work? QultureRocks. (n.d.). https://www.qulture.rocks/en/blog/360-degree-feedback-what-is-it-and-how-does-it-work/.

5 tips for building trust as a leader from astronaut, Brian Duffy. Experience to Lead. (2020, September 15). https://www.experiencetolead.com/5-tips-for-building-leader-trust/.

7 leadership risks you should be taking. Criteria For Success. (2020, April 21). https://criteriaforsuccess.com/7-leadership-risks-you-should-be-taking/.

Arnold, J. D. (2020, May 1). *Four reasons you need to be thinking about goal alignment.* Best Leadership Articles to Begin Developing Your Employees. https://blog.inspiresoftware.com/reasons-need-thinking-about-goal-alignment.

Beqiri, G. (2018, April 24). *360 degree FEEDBACK – DEFINITION, Benefits, process and examples.* VirtualSpeech. https://virtualspeech.com/blog/360-degree-feedback.

Four ways that 360 degree feedback Benefits Leaders. Explorance. (n.d.). https://explorance.com/blog/four-ways-that-360-degree-feedback-benefits-leaders-2/.

Google. (n.d.). *10 ways to make your Employees 10x more productive.* Google. https://www.google.com/amp/s/www.entrepreneur.com/amphtml/304220.

Google. (n.d.). *Council post: Seven Self-care strategies of successful leaders.* Google. https://www.google.com/amp/s/www.forbes.com/sites/forbescoachescouncil/2020/02/21/seven-self-care-strategies-of-successful-leaders/amp/.

Google. (n.d.). *How taking risks evokes leadership success.* Google. https://www.google.com/amp/s/m.huffpost.com/us/entry/10843744/amp.

Google. (n.d.). *How to develop your talent management strategy - hrd.* Google. https://www.google.com/amp/s/www.hrdconnect.com/2019/09/06/how-to-develop-your-talent-management-strategy/amp/.

Google. (n.d.). *The importance of risk taking in leadership – journey to leadership*. Google. https://www.google.com/amp/s/journeytoleadershipblog.com/2019/04/01/risk-taking-in-leadership/amp/.

Google. (n.d.). *Why team alignment is important for the organization*. Google. https://www.google.com/amp/s/blog.vantagecircle.com/team-alignment/amp/.

Great leaders take risks. SIGMA Assessment Systems. (2021, May 12). https://www.sigmaassessmentsystems.com/great-leaders-risk-taking/.

Heathfield, S. M. (n.d.). *360 degree Feedback: See the good, the bad and the ugly*. The Balance Careers. https://www.thebalancecareers.com/360-degree-feedback-information-1917537.

Heathfield, S. M. (n.d.). *360 degree Feedback: See the good, the bad and the ugly*. The Balance Careers. https://www.thebalancecareers.com/360-degree-feedback-information-1917537.

How to implement an organizational 360 feedback initiative. CCL. (2021, May 20). https://www.ccl.org/articles/leading-effectively-articles/how-to-implement-360-feedback-initiative/.

Jacob Morgan. (2020, October 27). *Why great leaders are risk-takers*. Medium. https://medium.com/jacob-morgan/why-great-leaders-are-risk-takers-22e031313391.

James, J. (2020, November 20). *Why training is essential to your talent management strategy*. Training Courses that Get Results. https://www.zandax.com/business-blog/why-training-is-essential-to-your-talent-management-strategy.

Jen Knox Shanahan Author Profile. (2018, May 16). *Leaders create SAFE Spaces: Lead read today*. Lead Read Today | Fisher College of Business. https://fisher.osu.edu/blogs/leadreadtoday/blog/leaders-create-safe-spaces.

Khan, N. (2019, July 21). *What is post traumatic stress disorder? 5 criteria, symptoms and treatment*. Betterhelp. https://www.betterhelp.com/advice/stress/what-is-post-traumatic-stress-disorder-dsm-5-criteria-symptoms-and-treatment/?utm_source=AdWords.

Khan, N. (2019, July 21). *What is post traumatic stress disorder? Dsm 5 criteria, symptoms and treatment*. Betterhelp. https://www.betterhelp.com/advice/stress/what-is-post-traumatic-stress-disorder-dsm-5-criteria-symptoms-and-treatment/?utm_source=AdWords&utm_medium=Search_PPC_m&utm_term=_b&utm_content=118051370367&network=g&placement=&target=&matchtype=b&utm_campaign=11771068538&ad_type=text&adposition=&gclid=CjOKCQjw0emHBhC1ARIsAL1QGNfrPsNEPhHpYP-nlaaiORV8dm8M4Ekk07NatSAkjRmaehKXftzTOEkaArMWEALw_wcB.

Lawler, M., Phillips, Q., Revelant, J., Millard, E., Landau, M. D., Lawler, M., & Russell, T. (n.d.). *What is self-care and why is it critical for your health?: Everyday health*. EverydayHealth.com. https://www.everydayhealth.com/self-care/.

Lynch, D. D. S. (2019, August 27). *5 reasons why team leadership is better than SOLO LEADERSHIP*. Smartt Strategies. https://www.smarttstrategies.com/blog/5-reasons-why-team-leadership-is-better-than-solo-leadership.

Manager, E. L. M. O. C. (2021, March 12). *7 benefits of having a talent management system*. ELMO Software AU. https://elmosoftware.com.au/resources/blog/7-benefits-of-having-a-talent-management-system/.

Mayo Foundation for Medical Education and Research. (2018, July 6). *Post-traumatic stress disorder (ptsd)*. Mayo Clinic. https://www.mayoclinic.org/diseases-conditions/post-traumatic-stress-disorder/symptoms-causes/syc-20355967.

MediLexicon International. (n.d.). *Post-traumatic stress disorder (ptsd): Symptoms, treatment, and more*. Medical News Today. https://www.medicalnewstoday.com/articles/156285.

Mentoring vs coaching: The key differences and benefits. PushFar. (n.d.). https://www.pushfar.com/article/mentoring-vs-coaching-the-key-differences-and-benefits/.

the Mind Tools Content Team   By the Mind Tools Content Team, Team, the M. T. C., wrote, B. T., & wrote, M. (n.d.). *What is leadership?* Leadership Skills Training from MindTools.com. https://www.mindtools.com/pages/article/newLDR_41.htm.

Morgan, J. (2020, January 13). *What is leadership, and who is a leader?* Chief Learning Officer - CLO Media. https://www.chieflearningofficer.com/2020/01/06/what-is-leadership-and-who-is-a-leader/.

NHS. (n.d.). *Causes Of Post Traumatic Stress Disorder*. Nhs choices. https://www.nhs.uk/mental-health/conditions/post-traumatic-stress-disorder-ptsd/causes/.

Parsloe, E., & Clutterbuck. (n.d.). *Everything you ever wanted to know about coaching and mentoring*. Coaching and Mentoring Network. https://new.coachingnetwork.org.uk/information-portal/what-are-coaching-and-mentoring/.

Ryba, K. (n.d.). *How to Align Individual, team, and organizational goals for success*. Employee Engagement Software. https://www.quantumworkplace.com/future-of-work/how-to-align-organizational-goals.

Top 10 ways to improve employee efficiency. Workest. (2021, May 14). https://www.zenefits.com/workest/top-10-ways-to-improve-employee-efficiency/.

U.S. Department of Health and Human Services. (n.d.). *Post-traumatic stress disorder*. National Institute of Mental Health. https://www.nimh.nih.gov/health/topics/post-traumatic-stress-disorder-ptsd/.

What does self-care look like for leaders? Investors in People. (2020, December 18). https://www.investorsinpeople.com/knowledge/what-does-self-care-look-like-for-leaders/.

What is 360 Degree feedback? custominsight. (n.d.). https://www.custominsight.com/360-degree-feedback/what-is-360-degree-feedback.asp.

What is posttraumatic stress disorder? What Is PTSD? (n.d.). https://www.psychiatry.org/patients-families/ptsd/what-is-ptsd.

What is talent management? Definition, process, and model. toolbox.com. (n.d.). https://www.toolbox.com/hr/talent-management/articles/what-is-talent-management/.

What is Talent management? Knowledge Anywhere. (n.d.). https://www.knowledgeanywhere.com/resources/article-detail/what-is-talent-management.

What is Talent MANAGEMENT? Model, Strategy, Process. Valamis. (n.d.).

https://www.valamis.com/hub/talent-management.

Wikimedia Foundation. (2021, March 24). *360-Degree feedback*. Wikipedia. https://en.wikipedia.org/wiki/360-degree_feedback.

www.ingramcontent.com/pod-product-compliance
Lightning Source LLC
Chambersburg PA
CBHW030331160726
47992CB00005B/2242